John Tullock

Corals

Everything about
Purchase, Care, Feeding,
and Compatibility

Filled with Full-color Photographs

Illustrations by
Michele Earle-Bridges

BARRON'S

CONTENTS

INTRODUCTION TO CORALS

Corals—Master Builders of the Sea

Many writers have called coral reefs "rain forests of the ocean." Created where suitable temperatures and an absence of sedimentation allow the nearly microscopic, free-swimming coral larvae to settle and grow, reefs have life spans measured in millennia. Individual coral organisms divide, each successive generation literally growing atop the skeletons of its ancestors. In this manner, over time, some species of corals form massive reefs. The Great Barrier Reef of Australia stretches over 620 miles (2,000 km) and is believed to be the largest structure created by living organisms on the planet. Numerous smaller reef systems occur throughout the tropics, as fringing and barrier reefs on the eastern coasts of continents and around archipelagos, and as atolls encircling what were once volcanic islands. Besides the corals themselves, thousands of species of fish, invertebrates, and seaweeds are associated with coral reefs, making them among the most biologically diverse of earth's ecosystems.

Blue water, colorful fish, and abundant life are found on the reef.

Corals rank high in popularity among marine aquarium hobbyists. Since the introduction of minireef aquariums in the 1980s, aquariums featuring corals have achieved a popularity that continues to grow. During the decade before 1997 the global trade in live stony corals increased tenfold. Most of this increase can be attributed to purchases by hobbyists of specimens for their minireefs.

Coral Conservation Issues

Corals of all types are now being propagated for the aquarium trade. In fact, the best choices among aquarium corals are those that reproduce themselves under captive conditions—such specimens have obviously demonstrated that they adapt to captivity. Usually, the requirements for their aquarium care have been worked out precisely by the propagator, who can share the information with customers.

Unfortunately, fewer than one percent of the coral colonies in international trade come from captive propagation. Therefore, it is often necessary to search a bit in order to find them. If you are lucky enough to have an aquarium club in your vicinity, joining it will put you in contact with hobbyists who share your interests and can provide a wealth of valuable tips, including sources for captive-propagated corals. You may even be able to trade coral fragments with them.

Because nearly all of the live corals available come from wild harvest, the question of the impact of this harvest upon coral reef ecosystems has arisen. For example, over one quarter of the total world trade in live stony corals consists of species for which mortality in the aquarium approaches 100 percent. Such non-adaptable corals challenge even the abilities of professional aquarists, and should be avoided by hobbyists, especially beginners. Clearly, the continued removal of these corals from wild habitats is a questionable practice.

Coral Farms

Most stony corals in the aquarium trade are imported from Indonesia. The collection of stony corals is already prohibited in many countries, including the United States, and the question of whether even abundant species should be collected for the aquarium is at present receiving intensive scrutiny. *Captive propagation* is widely considered to be the best alternative to wild harvest. Coral "farms" have sprung up all over the country, ranging in size from what can be accommodated in a basement to multimillion-dollar, highly sophisticated facilities. Cultivation of coral fragments in trays placed in shallow water is also being pursued in the tropical Indo-Pacific, in the Solomon Islands, for example. The supply of aquarium corals will one day perhaps come exclusively from such sources. I urge readers to take the extra trouble to locate propagated corals and to support propagators by purchasing their products.

Artificial Substrates

Billions of larval corals probably die for every one that finds a suitable spot and grows into a visible colony. Coral spawnings of many species occur seasonally and predictably, with the waters surrounding the reef becoming clouded with eggs and sperm. An idea that takes advantage of this phenomenon is the placement of artificial substrates, such as ceramic tiles, in hopes of collecting coral larvae that will grow into aquarium-size colonies. The "seeded" tiles could eventually be transferred to grow-out aquaria in which conditions could be adjusted to optimize their rate of growth, or could be moved to fenced-off lagoon areas where they might be conveniently tended. Upon reaching a suitable size, they could be sold to aquarists.

Aquaculture of Live Rock

Aquaculture of live rock, an infant industry developing in Florida in response to a ban on collecting natural rock, may give aquarists access to small colonies of Atlantic stony coals for the first time in many years. Colonies of stony coral that develop on cultured live rock will not disqualify the rock from being sold for aquarium use. Before this ruling, coral colonies could not be legally collected in Florida. Thus, the species occurring there were off limits to the aquarium trade. Similar restrictions apply throughout much of the Caribbean.

Hobbyists who begin only with captive-propagated specimens will not only be promoting ecologically sound practices, but also will be giving themselves an advantage in their culture. Beginners are more likely to make deadly mistakes, so it is unwise to "practice" on expensive, wild-collected specimens.

Further, a beginning hobbyist is likely to be more successful with a captive-propagated specimen than might be the case with its wild-caught counterparts, because precise instructions for maintaining captive-propagated corals are usually available from the producer. A description of the conditions under which a wild coral was growing at the time of its collection is seldom available, so providing appropriate conditions in the aquarium is a matter of making educated guesses. This is something experienced aquarists do better than novices.

The Coral Reef Aquarium

Corals may vary in their specific requirements, but it will quickly be appreciated that they can be successfully maintained in community aquariums. The obvious approach to structuring such a community is to keep species with similar needs together. For example, branching, rapidly growing corals such as *Acropora* and *Pocillopora* do best under intense illumination in turbulent water, because they grow on the reef crest where these conditions prevail. Species from a different habitat, however, may need dim light and may react negatively to heavy turbulence, or even be damaged by it.

For aquarium purposes, the term *coral* extends to a diversity of scientific classifications, or *taxa*. Scleractinians, hard corals that produce a skeleton of calcium carbonate and in some cases form massive reefs, are but one kind. Others discussed in this book are

✔ sea mats
✔ false corals
✔ stoloniferans
✔ leather corals
✔ gorgonians, and a few other taxa.

A complete classification of corals and their close relatives is found in the chapter Classification of Corals, beginning on page 49.

Five factors are important in the aquarium husbandry of corals:

1. Illumination, varying from bright in shallow, nearly transparent water, to dim in deep, turbid, or shaded areas

2. Water movement, ranging from almost calm in sheltered lagoons to heavy surf at the top of the outer reef crest

3. Chemical stability, essential for vital physiological processes

4. Avoidance of interspecific aggression, by means of which different corals inhibit the growth of competing species in the immediate vicinity

5. The ability of the aquarist to observe signs of trouble and to take appropriate action

Chemical stability results from proper testing and adjustments, as described in the chapter Marine Aquarium Basics, beginning on page 17. Troubleshooting information can be found in the chapter Caring for Corals, on page 73, and in more specialized references listed in the Information section, page 91. The remaining factors—illumination, water movement, and aggression—largely determine the specific environment, or "microhabitat" in which a particular species is most likely to thrive. These are covered in the species accounts beginning on page 49.

Much of the information presented in this book I acquired through personal experience, although the basic insights for the principles discussed have come from others, going all the way back to high school biology. A selection of recent books that are especially useful

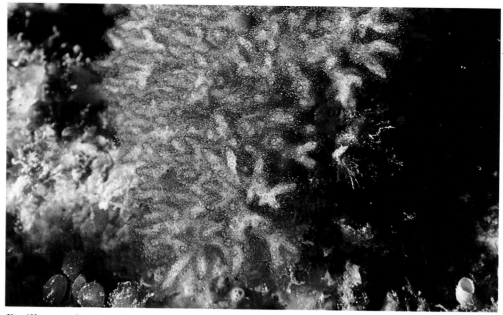

Pocillopora damicornis *is propagated for the aquarium trade.*

Cladocora arbuscula *colonies occur on live rock cultivated in Florida.*

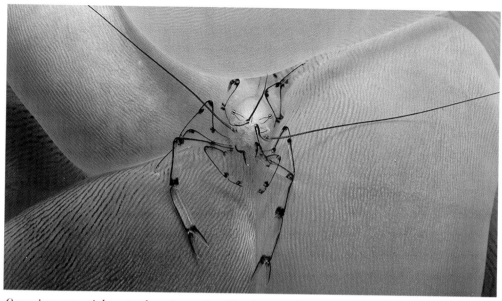

Organisms we might not otherwise notice, like the tiny shrimp among the tentacles of a bubble coral, can take center stage in the aquarium.

Blastomussa, a stony coral, grows well in calm, moderately shady conditions.

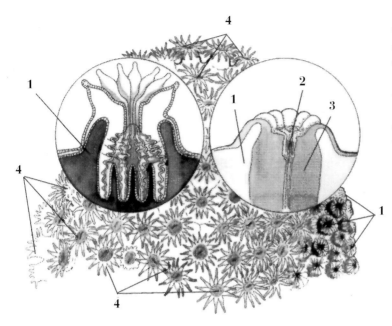

One of the many corals kept by hobbyists— stony coral.
1. Skeleton (corallum).
2. Gastrovascular cavity.
3. Polyp tissue.
4. Individual polyps in a shared corallum.

is included in the Information section (page 91). Besides books, countless letters, e-mails, presentations, and telephone calls from aquarium hobbyists, both novice and experienced, have provided me with a wealth of useful information. I am grateful for all of the help. This book is dedicated to hobbyists everywhere who invest extra effort to help others enjoy the fun and fascination of marine aquarium keeping.

As a general rule, the smaller the aquarium, the fewer the microhabitats that can be accommodated within it. Therefore, you must pay careful attention to the selection of species for a smaller aquarium. Also, the smaller the volume of water contained within the aquarium, the more difficult it becomes to maintain correct environmental parameters as the number of inhabitants increases. Beginners are, therefore, encouraged to start with a fairly large aquarium, of 50 to 100 gallons (189–378 L), and to focus on a selection of species that prefer approximately the same conditions. Do not make the mistake of choosing a 10-gallon (38 L) tank and stocking it with "one of everything."

Ideally, an aquarium for corals provides a glimpse of life on a real reef; the aquarium becomes a minireef. Minireef enthusiasts include in their aquariums not only corals but a variety of other invertebrates, seaweeds, and fishes, in an effort to simulate the mind-boggling biodiversity of a natural reef ecosystem. When well done, a minireef aquarium becomes a living work of art whose beauty evolves as the organisms grow and interact. Corals are long lived under proper care. A minireef can provide enjoyment and a daily learning experience for many years.

Things to Do Before Beginning Your Own Coral Aquarium

There are many important factors you should consider before beginning a coral aquarium.

✔ Talk to experienced hobbyists first. Not only can they provide you with a wealth of valuable information and tips, experienced coral aquarists can also alert you to potential problems that you may not have considered.

✔ Do research. Information is the key to success with any marine aquarium, and is especially important for an aquarist with an interest in corals. Turn to the Information section of this book (see page 91). You will find an extensive list of Internet sites, magazines, and books. These resources should answer most of your initial questions and provide access to still more detailed information.

✔ Visit aquarium supply shops. Talk to dealers and sales personnel, and begin to think about what you would like your coral aquarium to look like. Share your ideas, and ask whether they are feasible based on such factors as your budget and the time you plan to devote to your new hobby.

✔ Decide which species of coral you would like to keep. Keep coral conservation issues in mind (see page 5). Remember, while corals of all types are now being propagated for the aquarium trade, fewer than one percent of coral colonies in international trade come from captive propagation. Therefore, it may be necessary to search a bit in order to find the species you plan on keeping.

✔ Review your budget. Are you willing to spend the sums necessary in order to maintain a proper coral aquarium? Coral aquariums require various, and sometimes expensive, equipment, and other supplies. Some of these items include:

- Lighting systems
- Filtration systems
- Reverse osmosis units
- Powerheads
- Wavemakers
- Temperature control systems
- Water quality testing kits
- Chemical treatments to maintain water quality
- Aquarium décor accessories

✔ Finally, and most importantly, determine whether a coral aquarium is right for you. Before making a large investment of your time and money, decide whether you would find a coral aquarium a fulfilling and enjoyable hobby. Remember, keeping an aquarium is not the same as keeping a cat, dog, or even a snake. If, however, you believe a coral aquarium fits your lifestyle, you will find that maintaining a coral aquarium can be a fascinating and lifelong hobby with many rewards.

Peppermint shrimps, Lysmata wurdemanni, *are efficient scavengers that won't harm corals.*

The photosynthetic Caribbean sea fan, Gorgonia, *can grow to remarkable size.*

The red color form of Trachyphyllia geoffroyi.

Hobbyists seek out especially colorful forms of Acropora.

Zooxanthellae

The majority of corals of interest to aquarists have symbiotic dinoflagellates living within their tissues. These one-celled, photosynthetic organisms, known as "zooxanthellae," are essential for the corals' long-term survival in the aquarium. Understanding this was one of the advances that made minireef aquariums possible. As a rule, corals that lack zooxanthellae are among the more challenging aquarium subjects, because they require regular feeding with a substitute for the tiny organisms that constitute their natural diet. Beginners, therefore, should start only with zooxanthellate species. Because zooxanthellae are photosynthetic, they require light. Providing natural sunlight or, more commonly, satisfactory artificial lighting, is a key element in establishing an aquarium life-support system for photosynthetic corals.

Lighting Sources

Available lighting sources include both fluorescent and high-intensity systems, each with advantages and disadvantages.

In choosing aquarium lighting equipment for corals, five factors must be taken into account:

1. the area being illuminated

2. the depth of the water

3. the intensity of the light source

4. the spectrum of the light source

5. the photoperiod

Fluorescent Lighting

Fluorescent lighting is widely available, and is recommended for tanks up to 48 inches (122 cm) in length and 18 inches (46 cm) in depth, or 75 gallons (284 L) capacity. If ordinary standard-output (SO) lamps are used, two to four lamps are required. These must be of the maximum wattage—determined by the length of the tube—that can be accommodated across the top of the aquarium. For example, a 30-gallon (114 L) tank that is 36 inches (91 cm) in length can accommodate 30-watt SO lamps, which are also 36 inches in length. Fifteen-watt lamps are 18 inches (46 cm) in length, 20-watt lamps are 24 inches (61 cm) in length, and 40-watt lamps are 48 inches (122 cm) in length. Increased intensity can be obtained by using high-output (HO) and very high-output (VHO) fluorescent lamps, which use more electricity than SO lamps.

High-Intensity Lighting

Larger aquariums require high-intensity lighting. This may be provided by metal halide equipment. One 175-watt metal halide lamp provides sufficient illumination for an area of about 4 square feet (122 square cm), and up to a water depth of 24 inches (61 cm). For larger areas, more lamps are needed. Metal halide lamps generate heat and must be used in conjunction with a ventilation fan to prevent

Multiple lamp fluorescent lighting system.

overheating. Aquariums illuminated with metal halide systems may also need a *chiller* to prevent the water temperature from rising too high. Metal halide equipment can be used for smaller aquariums, and this will result in a higher light intensity, since the area illuminated is smaller. Overheating is more likely to be a problem with a smaller tank.

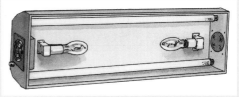

Metal halide lighting system.

Broad-Spectrum Lighting

Both red and blue light wavelengths are absorbed by chlorophyll, the chief photosynthetic pigment. Accessory pigments allow organisms to utilize light of other wavelengths, as well; therefore, broad-spectrum lighting that mimics natural sunlight is the best choice. Generally, choosing lamps with a strong blue component, indicated by a Kelvin temperature rating above 5000°, will provide sufficient light for coral growth. Kelvin temperature ratings are a convenient way to compare different light sources. As the light source becomes progressively more blue, or "actinic," the Kelvin temperature increases.

When planning an aquarium for corals, it is unlikely you will design the system with too much illumination. Specimens that prefer subdued lighting may be placed lower in the tank, or in a shaded spot. Specimens that require maximal exposure may be placed near the top of the tank. The dealer or propagator that provided your corals should be able to make specific lighting recommendations. When in doubt, choose more intense lighting.

Measuring Light Intensity

A photographic exposure meter can be used to measure light intensity. Focus a 35 mm camera on a sheet of white paper or a photographer's neutral gray card 18 inches (46 cm) below the light source you intend to use. Move in as close as your lens allows, while remaining in focus. Set the film speed at 125 ASA, and the shutter speed at 1/125 second; note the f-stop as indicated by the exposure meter. The light intensity in lumens (= footcandles) is equal to $20(f)^2$. Thus, at $f11$, the light source provides 2,420 lumens ($20 \times 11 \times 11 = 2,420$). Aim for an aquarium illumination intensity of 10,000 lumens per square meter (10.76 square feet) of surface area, if the aquarium is 24 inches (61 cm) or less in depth.

Photoperiod

Photoperiod, the length of the day, is also important for corals. Best results are obtained with a photoperiod of up to 14 hours, but no longer. I suggest a minimum of 10 hours. Use a timer to provide consistent control of the photoperiod. Some aquarists use multiple timers and a combination of fluorescent and metal halide lighting to provide a lower level of lighting (fluorescent only) early and late in the day, and a higher level (both fluorescent and metal halide) for several hours around midday. The goal of this arrangement is to simulate fluctuations in natural lighting. Timers are available at any hardware store or do-it-yourself center, as well as aquarium shops.

MARINE AQUARIUM BASICS

A suitable aquarium for corals provides adequate room, simulates conditions from the natural habitat of the coral, and continuously meets the physiological requirements of the inhabitants.

Water Quality

Strangely, aquarists do not give much thought to the quality of the water that they use to prepare synthetic seawater, but municipal tap water and well water should be purified for aquarium use, because of contaminants that can cause problems in the marine aquarium. Algae nutrients such as phosphate, toxic metals such as copper, and a host of other compounds may all be found in tap water. While these contaminants are present at levels considered safe for drinking, they are often too high for aquarium purposes.

Reverse Osmosis

For hobbyists with minimal water needs, the best bet may be to purchase distilled water from a supermarket. If you need large amounts of purified water, however, it is probably cheaper in the long run to purify tap water by reverse osmosis (RO). This technique uses

A minireef aquarium can be home to numerous corals, such as pulsing Xenia.

water pressure to force tap water through a special membrane, in effect "straining out" pollutants. RO units have two drawbacks: Water is produced drop by drop, with typical units producing about 15 to 25 gallons (57–95 L) of water per day. Thus, a reservoir is required. And, about 4 gallons (15 L) of wastewater are produced for every gallon (3.8 L) of product water. The wastewater can be used for cleaning or irrigation purposes, or for freshwater aquariums.

Deionization: If the source water contains unusually high levels of contaminants, some troublesome compounds, such as phosphate, may remain in the product water in an amount sufficient to cause problems in the aquarium, even though 99 percent is removed by the RO membrane. If this proves to be the case, RO water may need further purification by deionization. Deionization resins absorb undesired components from the water. The addition of a deionization filter to an RO system can result in purified water comparable to distilled water.

Deionization can also be used as the sole means of water purification, dispensing with RO altogether, but this is a more expensive option, as the resins must be replaced periodically. The advantages of using deionization alone are that water is produced on demand, rather than drop by drop, and there is no wastewater production.

Seawater Chemistry

Every marine aquarist must learn how to test aquarium water and to interpret the results.

Aquarists who intend to keep corals and other marine invertebrates may need to carry out the following tests:

✔ pH
✔ alkalinity
✔ ammonia
✔ nitrite
✔ nitrate
✔ phosphate
✔ calcium

Ammonia and nitrite tests are needed when establishing the biological filter system. These tests may also be helpful in diagnosing problems with an established aquarium. When something interferes with the biological filtration process, ammonia or nitrite, or both, can accumulate. Under normal circumstances, however, tests for these two compounds are not routinely performed. Similarly, phosphate testing is important in managing unwanted or excessive growth of algae. Since the kit is often considerably more expensive than the others listed, you may want to wait until you really do need a phosphate kit before you purchase one.

Regardless of which brands of test kits you buy, follow the instructions for their use. Always rinse test vials thoroughly with distilled water after each use, and rinse the vial with the water to be tested prior to each use. Do not store test reagents for more than a year.

Temperature

Temperature control is important for corals. The stabilizing effect of water's high specific heat—the heat required to change its temperature—means that seawater temperature in a given area fluctuates over a more narrow range than the surrounding air temperature.

Heaters: The aquarium may require a heater of sufficient wattage to keep the aquarium at a constant temperature of 74 to 82°F (24–28°C). Sometimes, heat from lights and pumps is enough to keep the tank within this range. If additional heat is required, about 3 watts per gallon is usually satisfactory. The higher the wattage, for a given number of gallons being heated, the faster the temperature of the water will rise when the heater is on. Sudden temperature shifts are to be avoided; therefore, do not select a heater that is of a higher wattage than that recommended. The heater must be shielded in some way to protect corals from contact. Despite the fact that the heater, while immersed, may feel only slightly warm to the touch, it can burn the delicate tissues of the cnidarian—that is, the living body of the coral.

Chillers: The aquarium may require a chiller if it does not remain below 82°F (28°C), except for brief periods. Chillers typically cost several hundred dollars. If necessary to keep the marine aquarium from overheating, however, a chiller is an indispensable component.

An aquarium chiller operates in the same way as a refrigerator or air conditioner. A refrigerant gas is compressed by an electrically driven compressor, which results in the gas losing energy—its temperature goes down. The compressed gas flows through a heat exchanger, where it picks up heat from the surrounding medium, in this case, water from the aquarium that is being pumped through the exchanger. The gas carries this heat back toward the compressor and, on the way, encounters an expansion valve, which allows the pressure to drop. As the pressure drops, the gas gives up heat to a radiator, which, in turn, dispels the heat into the surrounding air with the aid of a fan.

A chiller does not create cold; rather, it removes heat from the water. The rate at which a particular chiller removes heat determines its efficiency. Heat is measured in BTUs (British Thermal Units). One BTU is the amount of heat required to raise the temperature of one pound (0.45 kg) of water by 1°F (0.56°C). Thus, the higher the BTU rating of the chiller, the faster it will lower the temperature of a tank of a given size. A chiller with a high BTU rating will keep the tank at a constant temperature with less use of electricity and less wear and tear on the compressor than will a chiller of lower BTU rating. Unfortunately, often a particular chiller's BTU rating can be determined only in actual use, which is seldom practical if you are merely considering a purchase. Your dealer, or a chiller manufacturer, may be able to provide BTU rating information.

The calculated BTU rating for a 1/5 horse-power chiller was 2,800 BTU in a one-hour measuring period. I made the determination using a 120-gallon (454 L) aquarium system with metal halide lighting, two powerheads, and a 700 gallons per hour recirculating pump. This chiller adequately maintained the water temperature within one degree of the desired point, 78°F (26°C), while the ambient temperature ranged from 66°F to 84°F (19–29°C). The system remained stable over the course of a year, during which time it housed various invertebrates and fishes.

The most efficient chiller designs have a high BTU rating, do not feature a movable heat exchanger, and have sufficient capacity for the size tank on which they are installed.

Salinity

Measuring specific gravity with a hydrometer allows you to estimate the salinity of the water, if the temperature is also known. *Salinity* refers to the amount of dissolved solids (salts) in the water, and, in a typical sample of ocean water is 3.5 percent or 35 parts per thousand (ppt), usually written as 35‰. For water of a given salinity, the observed hydrometer reading will vary with the temperature. However, the observed hydrometer reading can be used to determine the density of the water if a temperature correction is made, and from the density, the salinity can be determined. Table 1 in the Appendix can be used to make the temperature conversion to density for any hydrometer reading. From Table 2 in the Appendix, the salinity can be determined once the density is known. As can be seen from Table 2, after temperature conversion, the *density* of the water in your aquarium should be 1.0260, which is the value for natural seawater (NSW) at a salinity of 35‰. The *specific gravity* of NSW after temperature conversion is 1.0270.

Much of the literature on marine aquariums provides recommendations for hydrometer readings without regard to the need for appropriate temperature conversions. Always read carefully the instructions that come with any hydrometer to determine its proper calibration and how to convert the observed reading to salinity.

Refractometers: Rather than using a hydrometer, one can determine salinity directly with a refractometer. Either instrument requires calibration with distilled water prior to testing a seawater sample. The density and specific gravity of pure water are both 1.000 (after appropriate temperature conversions) and the salinity is, of

Hydrometers and Thermometers

In addition to chemical test kits, purchase a hydrometer and a thermometer. The hydrometer and thermometer measure specific gravity and temperature, respectively. Both are of great importance to marine organisms.

course, 0‰. Salinity measurements can also be made electronically. Aquarium dealers who specialize in reef tanks often carry these instruments.

Distilled water: Maintaining an aquarium for corals requires that important chemical components of the water be kept within a certain range of concentrations. Because the concentrations reported in the literature for specific ions, usually in milligrams per liter (mg/L), are based upon full-strength seawater at a salinity of 35‰, you must either maintain the aquarium at this salinity or make appropriate extrapolations each time a water test for one of these components is carried out. It is simpler to maintain a constant salinity. Once the aquarium is established at 35‰, the salinity can be easily maintained by adding distilled water to compensate for evaporation, the chief cause of salinity fluctuation in a small aquarium. Mark the correct water level on the glass with a permanent marker, and add distilled or RO water when the level drops below the mark. I suggest a maintenance schedule that keeps salinity adjustments to a minimum, despite the fact that many marine organisms tolerate a range of salinities.

pH

The degree of acidity or alkalinity of the aquarium water is measured as pH. Seawater is alkaline, and has a pH of about 8.3. As acid is added to seawater, the pH drops, with the minimum acceptable reading being about 7.8 or so. Acid is a byproduct of the biological filtration process discussed in detail later (see page 23). In addition, when carbon dioxide is released into the water as a result of respiration by fishes or invertebrates, it reacts to form carbonic acid; thus, the tendency in any aquarium is toward a decline in pH. Maintaining a pH of 8.3 can be accomplished by regular water changes, or through the addition of buffering agents. Major changes in pH can have important physiological consequences for corals, although most successful mini-reef aquariums experience a daily cycle of minor pH fluctuations.

Alkalinity: Alkalinity—associated terms: buffer capacity, KH, carbonate hardness—is a measure of the resistance of the water to a change in pH as acid is added. It is expressed in "milliequivalents per liter" (meq/L). Marine aquariums should be maintained at about 3.5 meq/L or slightly greater. At this alkalinity level, it will be easier for the correct pH to be maintained.

Nutrient Ions

Nitrogen compounds: Ammonia, nitrite, and nitrate are the major *nutrient ions* produced in a marine aquarium. They are also components of the biological filtration process, which is essential to the survival of all aquarium inhabitants.

Proteins, found in every kind of food, are amino acid compounds. These eventually wind up either in the proteins of the animal that consumed the food or in the water as excreted ammonia. Fish and invertebrates do not tolerate large amounts of ammonia in the water.

Fortunately, nitrifying bacteria can be cultivated in the aquarium. These bacteria convert the ammonia into nitrite and then into nitrate. Tests for ammonia and nitrite are used to determine if these bacteria-mediated processes, known collectively as *biological filtration* (see page 23), are proceeding correctly. Tests for ammonia and nitrite should always be "zero," after a population of nitrifying bacteria is established in the aquarium.

Nitrate, the end product of biological filtration, is tolerated to varying degrees by marine

organisms. Tests for nitrate should be performed on a weekly basis. Water changes should be carried out with sufficient frequency and in sufficient amounts to keep the nitrate concentration rather low, around 20 mg/L or less nitrate ion (<5 mg/L nitrate-nitrogen).

Nitrate is not toxic to marine organisms in small amounts. The accumulation, or perhaps depletion, of other compounds as the result of insufficient water changes may be harmful to the aquarium's inhabitants. Such effects are often incorrectly attributed to nitrate. Nevertheless, nitrate accumulation can be a convenient indicator of the need to perform a partial water change.

This pair of golden banded shrimp **(Stenopus scutellatus)** *need a temperature between 74–82°F (23.1–27.5°C).*

Phosphate: Phosphate concentrations above the limit of detection for aquarium test kits (about 0.05–0.10 mg/L) are often associated

with "blooms" of algae. Algae are not necessarily harmful; however, if, for example, corals are being smothered by an algal mat, limiting the amount of phosphate in the water will be an important technique in controlling it.

Calcium: Natural seawater (NSW) contains about 400 mg/L of calcium. Chemical and biological processes in the aquarium reduce its concentration over time. Adding a calcium supplement is necessary to maintain the calcium concentration.

Record Keeping

It is important to buy good test equipment, use it on a regular basis, and keep a written record of the results. Record the following information about the aquarium in a log book:
✔ date
✔ test(s) performed and results
✔ supplement(s) added and amount(s)
✔ temperature
✔ salinity
✔ amount of water changed
✔ species and size of animals added
✔ incidents of death or disease, treatments, and results
✔ additional observations

Nutrient Management

When you think about filtration equipment for any marine aquarium, think about nutrients. Since the waters surrounding coral reefs contain a paucity of nutrients, most of what one does in caring for a marine aquarium is basically nutrient removal.

Nutrients are, of course, essential for living organisms. Marine organisms have developed extremely efficient ways to capture, and in many cases to recycle, nutrients, with the result that the bulk of the nitrogen, phosphorus, and organic carbon present in tropical marine habitats is in the biomass, not dissolved in the water. In the aquarium, nutrients accumulate from the moment living organisms are added. This accumulation results in a decline in what aquarists collectively describe as the *water quality* of the system. If nothing is done to reverse this process, water conditions will deteriorate and the organisms will experience stress. Some effort is necessary to prevent, or at least retard, this worsening of water conditions. A set of techniques, collectively termed *filtration*, combined with water changes and the judicious application of chemical

Keeping a record of observations often helps spot trouble in time to take corrective action.

Schematic representation of the nitrogen cycle.

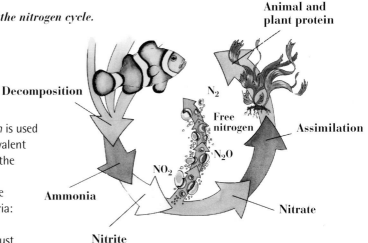

additives, enables the aquarist to maintain aquarium
water in good condition.

Biological Filtration

The term *biological filtration* is used
to describe the aquarium equivalent
of a natural process known as the
Nitrogen Cycle. The chemical
conversions associated with the
process are mediated by bacteria:
the nitrifiers, denitrifiers, and
heterotrophs. Every aquarist must
understand biological filtration: ammonia
excreted by fish and invertebrates is
oxidized to nitrite, and then to nitrate,
by nitrifying bacteria.

Ammonia is toxic to aquatic organisms at
levels that are barely detectable on a hobbyist-
type test kit. On the other hand, nitrate in
similarly low concentrations is harmless.

Nitrate may stimulate calcium uptake in
corals, making more frequent addition of calcium supplements necessary. The formation of
nitric acid from nitrate lowers alkalinity, as well.

The overall chemical formula for biological
filtration is:

$$2NH_3 + 3O_2 \longrightarrow 2NO_3^- + 6H^+$$

ammonia   oxygen   nitrate   hydrogen
                                   ions

Mineralization: Aquariums designed to
exhibit marine organisms are commonly
equipped with biological filters designed to
encourage colonization by nitrifying bacteria.
All of these systems focus upon rapid conversion of ammonia to nitrate. In them, mineralization of nutrients occurs—nitrogen that enters
the system as complex organic molecules (proteins) in food is reduced to its simpler, mineral
components by biological activity.

Heterotrophs: Not all of this biological
activity comes from animal metabolism of the
introduced food. In fact, only a small portion
of the food entering the aquarium is utilized
by the larger inhabitants, even if they eat it all.
Uneaten food and animal wastes can be utilized by microorganisms collectively termed
heterotrophs. The substances upon which heterotrophs feed may have been, like feces, previously processed by another organism or
group of organisms before the heterotrophs
can utilize them. The excretory products of
these larger organisms are then further acted
upon by microcrustaceans, nematodes, worms,
fungi, and protozoans, and finally reach the
heterotrophic bacteria. All along the way,
gases, minerals, trace elements, and various
organic compounds are being spewed out,

Sun zoanthids, **Palythoa grandis,** *like all corals must have water of the correct salinity.*

recycled, converted and reconverted in a whirl of biochemical activity. The end result consists primarily of ammonia, phosphate, sulfate, and carbon dioxide. The ammonia is utilized by nitrifying bacteria, which take oxygen from the surrounding water to oxidize ammonia to nitrite, extracting energy in the process. Additional nitrifiers oxidize nitrite to nitrate, also obtaining energy. These processes require oxygen, and all are said to be *oxidizing* reactions. What remains of the complex food molecules at the end of this process is about what would be left after burning them: water, carbon dioxide, and minerals.

Live rock: Because ammonia is toxic to all life forms except the nitrifiers (and algae), nitrogen management is vital to the survival of all the other organisms in the aquarium. The primary source of biological filtration in the aquarium is live rock—chunks of rock, taken from the ocean with various species of encrusting organisms attached. After collection, the rock is wrapped in wet newspaper and shipped in insulated cartons via air freight. It will first arrive in the hands of a broker who takes care of the import paperwork before shipping the rock to the retailer. Along the way, the rock remains in the original packing container; much depends upon how expeditiously the journey can be completed. Variations in transit time can have profound effects on the survival of organisms associated with the rock, in particular, larger species such as encrusting sponges or embedded mollusks.

Turbinaria and other stony corals cannot tolerate poor water conditions.

As common sense would suggest, the longer the rock is out of water, the fewer survivors.

Many of the organisms that were originally present on the rock are, surprisingly, able to survive the shipping process. In particular, beneficial bacteria and other microbes are retained. The fact that highly successful miniature reef aquariums can be created by relying on live rock as the sole source of biological filtration is strong evidence for the important role of live rock microfauna and -flora.

What exact role, if any, the great variety of live rock organisms may play in the ecology of the aquarium has yet to be determined. One can suggest several possible benefits, however, from rock that has a full, natural complement of life forms present:

1. The encrusting fauna of live rock assist in nutrient management in the aquarium, by sequestering nutrients within the biomass rather than having these same compounds available as particulate or dissolved substances in the water.

2. Another possible benefit is the production, almost continuously in some species, of the larvae that constitute the tank's plankton. These can be an important food source for filter-feeding invertebrates.

3. A significant benefit is the inherent stability created in a system that is highly diverse. Diverse systems seem better able than simpler ones to weather stress. While the typical aquarium may contain, for example, 40 species of algae, invertebrates and fish, the species on a single piece of live rock, when all the bacteria, protozoa, and microinvertebrates are counted, can number in the hundreds. The live rock fauna thus contribute significantly to the biodiversity of the aquarium. For more on using live rock, see page 43.

Denitrification

The chemical breakdown of complex organic matter by the action of heterotrophs is an essential step in the aquarium's nitrogen cycle. Another process, involving another specialized group of bacteria and operating in the absence of oxygen, is similarly important. This process is called *denitrification*. Denitrifying bacteria reduce nitrate to nitrogen gas, which escapes to the atmosphere. Bacteria living in the interior spaces of live rock carry out denitrification, and similar bacterial colonies can be encouraged to form in the substrate on the bottom of the tank. This layer is commonly described as live sand. The overall chemical reaction for the denitrification process is:

$$2NO_3^- + 6H^+ \longrightarrow N_2 + 3H_2O$$

nitrate   hydrogen   nitrogen   water
      ions   gas

Live sand: Live sand is analogous to live rock in that its incorporation into the system fosters natural, bacteriological processes within the aquarium. Dr. Jean Jaubert of Monaco originally investigated live sand, and his work has been expanded upon by scores of aquarium hobbyists. Jaubert's methods were first described in a major American hobbyist magazine by Sprung and Delbeek (1990). In brief, this technique relies upon a thick layer of sand on the aquarium bottom to provide an appropriate home for

denitrifying bacteria. A 2- to 3-inch (5–7 cm) layer of sand is seeded with live sand collected from the ocean floor. Small organisms present in the upper layers of the sand help to keep the substrate biologically active, while denitrifying bacteria thrive in the low-to-zero oxygen conditions in the deeper layers. This technique appears not only to result in denitrification; it appears also that the dissolution of the aragonite (calcium carbonate) returns both calcium and carbonate ions to the water. Dr. Jaubert has been successful in maintaining high levels of calcium and alkalinity in his systems, together with low levels of phosphate and nitrate, through reliance on these natural processes alone. For more on live sand, see page 43.

Photosynthesis

Another vital biochemical process that occurs in all ecosystems is photosynthesis. Photosynthesis is essential to many of the species in the marine aquarium, including most corals. On the other hand, some photosynthetic organisms, such as certain types of algae, can be a problem for the aquarist.

Photosynthetic organisms utilize light energy to power the reverse of the oxidation process, reduction. During photosynthesis, carbon dioxide is reduced to carbohydrate molecules in the presence of light. After nightfall, the energy stored in the carbohydrate molecules is liberated once again, using oxygen, in the same metabolic process used by nonphotosynthetic organisms to carry out decomposition. The energy liberated from carbohydrates is used by the photosynthesizer ultimately to create complex molecules for growth, development, reproduction, and other important biological tasks. When photosynthesizers are eaten by animals, or decomposed by bacteria or fungi, the energy stored in carbohydrates is liberated for the benefit of the consumers. Photosynthesis thus channels the sun's energy into the ecosystem.

Zooxanthellae: The role of bacteria in nitrogen utilization is important to the stability of the aquarium, but is likely to be quickly overshadowed by photosynthesis when phosphate and nitrate are abundant. Photosynthesizers absorb nitrogen compounds in the form of molecular nitrogen, ammonia, nitrite, and nitrate, and use them in the manufacture of proteins. Many corals depend upon photosynthesis because they host symbiotic algae, called *zooxanthellae*. These have important functions in the life of the coral, one of which is assimilation of waste products of the animal's metabolism. Much nutrient recycling thus occurs as a result of the symbiotic relationship. Probably, little ammonia is excreted into the water by organisms harboring photosynthetic symbionts. Tridacnid clams, for example, extract ammonia and nitrate from aquarium water. This is a most unanimal-like thing to do, and is, in fact, mediated by the symbiotic algae living in the clam's mantle tissues (Heslinga et al., 1990).

Biomass: In addition to species that are photosynthetic themselves or that have photosynthetic symbionts, the biomass of the marine aquarium consists of nonphotosynthetic invertebrates and microorganisms, such as protozoans, fungi, and heterotrophic bacteria. Any of these may release ammonia and other compounds into the water. However, it is fish, with their greedy appetites and high levels of activity, that provide most of the waste products. Interest in maintaining large numbers of fish no doubt led early marine aquarists to focus on the oxidation of ammonia to nitrate as the most important detoxification process that should take place in the aquarium system.

Filters: Both the design of the aquarium system and its maintenance must take into consideration biological filtration, denitrification, photosynthesis, and assimilation. Wet/dry filters, for example, are fine for achieving biological filtration, but a tank so equipped may develop excessive algae if no effort is made to reduce the accumulation of nitrate and phosphate. Artificial methods can be used to remove organic compounds before they are mineralized. The technique that best accomplishes this is foam fractionation, also known as protein skimming, discussed in the next section.

Assimilation: In addition, husbandry practiced by the aquarist must be directed toward minimizing the input of nutrients from outside the system, and exporting nutrients through regular removal of detritus and algae. Ideally, bacteria associated with live rock and live sand carry out both mineralization (nitrification) and denitrification. Growth of certain types of algae is allowed to develop naturally, permitting assimilation to occur. When all of these efforts work in concert, the system develops an equilibrium, and the water chemistry remains relatively stable, as in the sea.

A stable population: In a system that has been running for a year or more with no additions of new animals, there is little change in biomass. A stable population of nitrifying bacteria will convert any ammonia not collected by photosynthetic organisms; nitrate is converted to nitrogen by denitrifying bacteria or used by algae. When equilibrium exists, the net amount of measurable nitrogen as ammonia, nitrite, and nitrate will be near zero.

Consider what happens when a small fish dies. The fish's biomass is rapidly transformed. Through the action of scavengers, microinvertebrates, heterotrophic bacteria, and fungi, the nitrogen stored in the fish is now released all at once into the system. Ammonia, nitrite, and nitrate may all appear in the water, because the bacterial population is not large enough to take advantage quickly of the newly available food supply. Organic matter and phosphate are also released, fueling a noticeable surge in microalgae growth. The inexperienced aquarist may react to these changes with panic, taking all sorts of measures to restore the system to its former state. Removing any noticeable organic debris, changing some of the water, and persevering with routine care are all that need be done, however. A healthy system will return to equilibrium on its own in a few weeks, and the inhabitants will usually be able to weather the transient perturbations of their environment.

In my frequent correspondence with marine aquarists the world over, I am repeatedly surprised by the number of things that are added to, or done to, aquariums in an effort to avoid water changes or other maintenance chores. Undefined mixtures touted with vague claims of efficacy against a variety of problems, or as miraculous growth stimulants, are dumped into tanks, changing the environment in unknown ways and creating possibly stressful conditions

Biological filtration keeps water free of ammonia, which is toxic to **Lobophytum** *and other soft corals.*

Live rock is often encrusted with colorful coralline algae.

with which the organisms in the aquarium have no choice but to cope, or die.

Microorganisms—bacteria, fungi, algae, protozoans, and tiny invertebrates—are an important component of the aquarium community. Just as certain essential processes mediated by soil microorganisms sustain terrestrial communities of plants and animals, so does an invisible community of microorganisms sustain the aquarium. We add fertilizer to the garden patch in the form of manure or compost; organisms growing in the soil then transform nutrients contained in these fertilizers, performing chemical alterations that make the nutrients available to the plants growing in the garden. Gardeners appreciate this relationship between dead and living organic matter. Aquarists should, as well.

Dissolved Organic Carbon Removal

Protein skimming, also known as *foam fractionation*, works together with beneficial organisms to help maintain a low concentration of dissolved organic matter. Beneficial organisms assimilate organic molecules; protein skimmers remove them physically from the water. All skimmers work on the same principle:

1. Tank water is mixed with fine air bubbles, creating foam.

2. Organic matter dissolved in the water tends to collect on the surfaces of the bubbles.

3. As the foam builds up, it rises to the top of the skimmer, and spills over into a collection cup, eventually filling the cup with a greenish-brown, slightly viscous liquid that can be periodically discarded.

My experience has been that the recommendations made by skimmer manufacturers regarding the size of tank for which the skimmer is appropriate are generally reliable. When in doubt, buy a larger model. It is not possible to "over-skim" the aquarium; even a small, inefficient skimmer is probably better than none at all. Just make sure that you carefully follow the manufacturer's instructions regarding how to install and operate the skimmer.

The skimmer should be adjusted so that foam, not water, collects in the cup. It may take multiple adjustments over several days to achieve the desired result. I find that beginners typically set the air supply flow rate too high, so that clear water, not greenish, viscous foam, collects in the cup. Start with a setting that seems too low at first, and note how the waste accumulates after a few days. If the tank is new, little may collect, because only a small amount of material is present for the skimmer to remove. This does not indicate that something is wrong with the skimmer, only that the water does not contain much organic matter.

Detritus and Water Changes

All any filtration system can do is extend the useful life of the water in the tank. No filtration system can eliminate the need for partial water changes. All filtration methods are applied with the intent of preventing changes in the aquarium water that would render it unsuitable—stress producing—for the inhabitants of the tank. After 20 years of experience

with marine aquariums, I have concluded that a natural system is the best way to go.

Natural filtration is an ideal approach for the beginning aquarist, because most of the crucial work is carried out by living organisms, through the same processes that have evolved over eons and that continue to operate today in natural ecosystems. The only pieces of equipment required are the relatively simple devices needed to create water movement, to provide light, and to control temperature.

Only recently in the development of methods for successful maintenance of small marine aquariums has the importance of the sand or detritus microhabitats been recognized. Early efforts at creating coral reef aquariums stressed removal of every bit of accumulated detritus, and the elimination of any sort of substrate material on the tank bottom, as an aid to cleaning. Anyone who has ever explored the real ocean floor, even if only a few feet beyond the low tide line, knows that sand, mud, silt, and detritus, or some combination of these materials, is always present. We now know that beneficial organisms living in sand and detritus may assist in nutrient management. Thus, aquariums now have sandy floors, and hobbyists are not so meticulous about detritus removal. Removal of detritus should nevertheless be done periodically. A hand-held powerhead can be used to direct a stream of water into recesses where detritus accumulates, stirring up the particles and permitting them to be drawn into the filter. A canister filter with polyester pads, sponge, or a similar medium can be used to supplement temporarily the main filtration system in order to remove as much particulate matter as possible. A major cleaning such as this should be done every six months. The procedure mimics the effects of a tropical storm on a natural reef, leading some hobbyists to refer to it as giving the tank the "hurricane treatment."

Aquarists have traditionally paid the most attention to technological aspects of filtration system design, in an often futile effort to achieve artificially what can be more easily done by allowing "Nature to take its course" in the aquarium environment, and by following simple maintenance procedures such as adding calcium supplement and changing water. Much more attention is now paid to maintaining the measurable chemical and physical parameters of the seawater through simple, straightforward, manual procedures than to installing elaborate equipment.

Accessories

Corals have some special needs. A basic aquarium for them should include temperature control, appropriate lighting, and pumps to create water movement. In such a system, appropriately maintained, the aquarist can keep a remarkable variety of species. Additional labor-saving devices, such as timers for the lighting system or an electronic pH monitor, may make caring for the aquarium less time-consuming, but should not be considered as substitutes for the attention from the aquarist that any successful minireef must receive.

You will need an assortment of accessories for aquarium maintenance chores. Items that will be in contact with aquarium water should be labeled and used only for this purpose, to avoid inadvertently contaminating the aquarium. I suggest treating aquarium equipment as you would treat food-handling equipment.

By the same token, if you would consider a particular container suitable for food storage, it should also be acceptable for storing aquarium water, dry salt mix, and so on. Here is a suggested list of maintenance equipment:

✔ Five-gallon (19 L) buckets.

✔ Plastic containers of 30 to 50 gallons (114–189 L), for mixing and storing seawater. Plastic garbage cans work well; choose one with a snug-fitting lid.

✔ About 6 feet (1.8 m) of clear vinyl hose, for use as a siphon. (Aquarium shops carry siphons fitted with a funnel-like accessory that is very useful for removing lightweight material, such as fine detritus, without also removing the aquarium substrate.)

✔ Clear, rectangular plastic containers of various sizes for capturing and moving aquarium specimens. Do not use nets for moving corals, or any other marine fish or invertebrate, as the organism may become entangled. Also avoid removing organisms from the water. Many can survive out of water briefly, but it is still wise to keep them submerged when transferring from one tank to another.

Electronic Monitoring Devices

Digital electronic controllers are available to monitor and control aquarium equipment. Of most obvious use are timer programs that control lighting systems and switch pumps on and off to simulate turbulence. Some devices can also thermostatically maintain temperature within a narrow range by controlling both the aquarium heater and the chiller, and furthermore allow measurement of pH to be carried out continuously. In fact, any water property that can be detected with an electronic sensor is potentially subject to electronic monitoring.

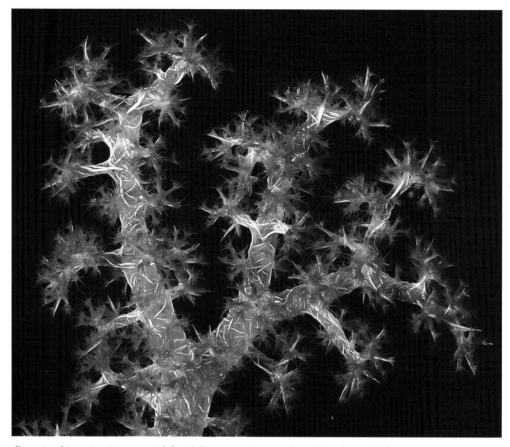

Protein skimming is essential for delicate species, such as **Dendronephthya.**

While electronic monitoring devices are probably of greatest value in commercial facilities with many tanks, home hobbyists have found that automation has its advantages. Units that can be linked to a personal computer are especially useful, in my experience, and can not only log aquarium data over time but also manipulate the information and display it in a variety of graphic formats. This makes keeping track of aquarium data a simple matter.

Advertising has apparently led some hobbyists to the conclusion that the more equipment involved in the aquarium system, the better. However, I find that the opposite is true. If the recommendations made in this chapter are followed, anyone can create and maintain a habitat suitable for the majority of marine species that are suitable for home aquariums without a great amount of gadgetry.

Above: Detritus should not be allowed to accumulate on this Platygyra, *or on other corals.*
Right: Tridacna maxima, *a giant clam.*
Below: Pachyclavularia (Briareum viridis) *spreads rapidly under good aquarium conditions.*

My procedure for aquarium monitoring can best be described as "test and tweak." I perform chemical tests for important parameters usually on a weekly basis, and then I "tweak" the water conditions back into line when any readings are found to be straying away from optimal levels.

Temperature

The temperature of the aquarium should be checked every time you are near the tank. Overheating can quickly kill all the inhabitants. Chilling is not likely to occur, except in the case of a wintertime power failure that leaves your home unheated. In this unfortunate circumstance, covering the aquarium with quilts or blankets may help prevent a serious temperature drop, but be sure to remove this insulation at once when power is restored.

Salinity

The rate at which water evaporates from the aquarium will vary with ambient conditions of temperature, humidity, ventilation and other factors, and so is difficult to predict. As water evaporates, the seawater in the tank becomes more salty. Weekly checks with a hydrometer should be done to insure that the salinity does not rise above 36‰ (see the tables on page 82 for conversion of hydrometer readings to salinity). Add distilled or RO water (*not* seawater) to compensate for evaporation, restoring the salinity to 35‰. Don't wait until the amount of replacement water needed is more than 10 percent of the tank volume, or you risk damage to the aquarium's inhabitants.

Nitrate Tests

A weekly nitrate test is the best way to insure that inputs of food are balanced by the bacterial activities collectively known as biological filtration. A rise in nitrate ion level above the typical baseline for your aquarium, usually about 20 mg/L, calls for an investigation into the source of the accumulation. Generally, a water change can be performed, using previously prepared and stored artificial

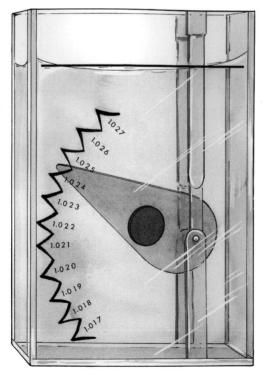

A hydrometer.

Test kits.

seawater, to reduce the nitrate concentration to the desired level. For example, if the reading is 40 mg/L, changing half the water would reduce the level to 20 mg/L.

Additional Tests

Other tests that should be performed weekly are pH, alkalinity, and calcium concentration. Since the pH can fluctuate over the course of a day, it is important that pH measurements always be taken at the same time of day. An abnormal pH reading should prompt the aquarist to investigate the cause. Poor aeration, for example, can cause the pH to fall, while the addition of too much limewater (see below) can cause the pH to rise.

Alkalinity and calcium are maintained at optimal levels (see Marine Aquarium Water Quality Parameters on page 81) by the addition of chemical agents such as limewater, or another supplement. Aquarists often use automated systems to add limewater to the tank. Developing a set procedure, either automated or manual, usually results in stable pH, alkalinity, and calcium levels. Limewater is made by combining calcium oxide with water to produce a saturated solution. A rounded teaspoon of calcium oxide will make a gallon (3.8 L) of limewater. Calcium oxide can be purchased from an aquarium dealer. Your dealer may also offer other products for maintaining calcium and alkalinity levels.

CORALS FOR THE MARINE AQUARIUM

For purposes of this book, the term *coral* includes all anthozoans other than sea anemones. True corals, the scleractinians, produce a calcified skeleton in which each *polyp* sits in its own cup, or corallite. The corallite is divided radially by septa. In the non-scleractinians that produce calcified skeletal structures, the cups supporting the individual polyps lack septa. In some anthozoans, the skeleton is composed of separate elements, or is absent entirely. While none of these other anthozoans would be called corals by a marine biologist, the similarities in their aquarium husbandry have led to their inclusion here.

Coral Aggression

Corals compete with each other for space on the reef. Defenses, including the ability to sting other corals, have evolved variously to enable corals to protect themselves from encroachment by competitors. For example, many produce sweeper tentacles, armed with stinging cells, that can reach several inches beyond the edges of the colony. Contact by a different species of coral may result in its

Beginning hobbyists may want to avoid species that do not adapt well to the aquarium.

being stung. Even among corals that do not possess sweeper tentacles, contact with another species may result in one being stung by the other. In the species descriptions in the next chapter, an attempt has been made to describe the degree of aggressiveness that a species is likely to exhibit toward its fellow aquarium inhabitants. No effort has been made, however, to predict the outcome of all possible interactions between the species described, so these aggressiveness rankings are only guidelines.

Place corals in the aquarium with several inches of space between each one and its neighbors. As the corals grow and come into contact, observe carefully for negative interactions. Prune or relocate specimens to eliminate contact where necessary. Portions that you remove may be used to establish new colonies (see the information on propagating corals on page 78).

In the discussion of anthozoans in the next chapter, the various groups are arranged in phylogenetic order, following the classification scheme used by Charles Delbeek and Julian Sprung (1994, 1997). In addition to the scientific name, common names are included for some species. While the use of scientific names exclusively would be preferable, many dealers in corals use common names; therefore, knowing which common names are sometimes applied should be helpful.

Suggested Coral Communities

While the species of corals available to mini-reef enthusiasts can be arranged in an infinite variety of combinations, the most successful aquarists exhibit together species originating from similar habitats. In this way, conditions of light intensity and water movement, two primary factors distinguishing different types of coral communities, can be adjusted to a particular regimen.

Two examples will serve to demonstrate how an aquarium design can reflect a particular microhabitat suited to one group of corals.

A Reef Crest Aquarium

The crest of a reef is sometimes exposed to the air at low tide. Corals found at such shallow depths are adapted to strong sunlight, high turbulence, and abundant oxygen. They are often broken by powerful wave action, and the fragments of many species are capable of regenerating new colonies. This characteristic makes several of them ideal candidates for propagation by aquarists. Among the available genera, *Acropora*, with numerous species, is common in reef crest habitats and elsewhere. Specimens often have attractive pigmentation that is thought to protect them from the effects of intense solar radiation.

Another genus that does well under similar conditions is *Pocillopora*, such as *P. damicornis*. *Stylophora pistillata* also prefers brilliant illumination and strong surge. A community of these corals should thrive in a relatively shallow tank of about 50 gallons (189 L), illuminated with two or more metal halide lamps. Turbulence should be vigorous. This can be provided by small submersible pumps, or power-heads, that are alternately switched on and off. A device known as a wavemaker is used to control the pumps automatically.

A Lagoon Aquarium

Lagoons are formed behind the protection of a reef, and are thus frequently rather shallow areas of comparatively quiet water. Sand or silt often covers the bottom. Because of the easy accessibility to collectors and the abundance of corals found in shallow water, many aquarium specimens are collected from this habitat. Among the stony corals, *Catalaphyllia* and *Euphyllia* may be found in lagoons. The former, more tolerant of sediments, is found in areas where silt accumulates, but need not grow on silt in the aquarium. Popular soft corals, including *Sarcophyton*, *Lobophytum*, and *Sinularia*, as well as sea mats and various corallimorphs, are found here. Red and green macroalgae, including some interesting forms that secrete calcified skeletons, can also be included in a lagoon aquarium. For this type of system, the water movement need not be so vigorous as that for a reef crest tank, but lighting should nevertheless be intense.

Enriching the Aquarium Community

After settling on an appropriate overall theme for the aquarium and choosing the corals that will go in it, one can proceed to select other organisms to enrich the aquarium community. As with corals, choose species suited to the habitat you are trying to model. For example, in the lagoon aquarium mentioned above, the orange-tailed blue damselfish, *Chrysiptera cyanea*, would be perfectly at home, while acanthurids such as the regal tang, *Paracanthurus hepatus*, would be better suited to the reef crest aquarium. Reference books that contain ecological information for a particular reef area are the best sources for matching the fish and invertebrates one sees in shops with their appropriate microhabitats. In this regard, a particularly good book that includes many popular aquarium fish is *Micronesian Reef Fishes*, by R. F. Myers (see Information, page 91).

Companions for Corals

Since one goal of the minireef aquarist is imitation of a natural habitat, it follows that fish, invertebrates, and seaweeds are appropriate tankmates for corals. However, some of the organisms you might see in the local aquarium shop will eat, damage, or smother corals. Following are general guidelines about the kinds of creatures that are the best companions for corals. It is always a good idea to check with the dealer about the compatibility of any potential introductions to an established coral community tank.

Fish

Certain fish are to be avoided because they are either potential predators of smaller members of the community, or are merely too large and rambunctious. Eliminating fish such as sharks, groupers, triggerfish, and larger members of other families still leaves plenty of choices, however.

As with the corals themselves, fish for the coral aquarium, especially in the hands of a

beginning hobbyist, should come from captive propagation sources, rather than the ocean. This is because captive-propagated fish, never having known any environment but the aquariums in which they were raised, adapt more readily to home aquariums and to foods that hobbyists can provide without too much trouble.

Anemonefish: Among the available species, the anemonefish, Family Pomacentridae, have been popular for many years. In addition, they are inexpensive and extremely hardy. Although the occasional anemonefish may take up residence among the polyps of a coral, irritating it and necessitating removal of one or the other, amenonefish seldom cause problems. It is not necessary to maintain the fish with a host anemone, although the anemones often do well under conditions similar to those required by corals. Hobbyists with an interest in anemonefish should obtain the companion volume in this series, *Clownfishes and Sea Anemones: A Complete Pet Owner's Manual*, which, along with numerous other good books, provides additional information on this fascinating group.

Dottybacks: Dottybacks, Family Pseudochromidae, are small sea basses sporting attractive coloration and perky dispositions. They seldom exceed 4 inches (10 cm) in length, and several species are available from hatcheries. Popular ones include the neon dottyback, *P. aldebarenesis*, the orchid dottyback, *P. fridmani*, and the sunrise dottyback, *P. flavivertex*. These all come from the Red Sea, Indian Ocean, and Persian Gulf. Still regularly collected in Indonesia and nearby locations in the Indo-Pacific region are the strawberry (*P. porphyreus*), crowned (*P. diadema*), and bicolor (*P. paccagnellae*) dottybacks with, respectively, solid purple, yellow

Although corals can sting, the tiny **Periclimenes pedersoni** *shrimp lives unharmed among the tentacles.*

Cleaner shrimp, Lysmata amboinensis, will not harm coral polyps.

with purple crown, and yellow plus purple coloration.

Fairy basslets: Related to the dottybacks are the fairy basslets, found, often in deeper waters, in the Caribbean region. At the time of this writing, none of these species was being hatchery-produced. The royal gramma, *Gramma loreto*, bearing the same color scheme as the bicolor dottyback, looks as if a yellow fish had been held by the tail and dipped in purple paint. These two species are easily distinguished, however, by the shape of the body

TIP

The Stinging Abilities of Corals

Remember when combining corals with other organisms to consider the stinging abilities of the corals. Some predatory species, such as the giant mushroom coral, *Amplexidiscus*, are capable of catching and eating small fish. Further, aggression between different species of corals and other cnidarians can result in specimen damage or loss. Space individuals so as to avoid contact and to allow room for growth.

and fins. Related species are the black-capped basslet, *G. melacara*, and the rare and expensive swissguard basslet, *Liopropoma rubre*.

Gobies: The goby clan offers many good fish for the coral aquarium. This group encompasses several families with numerous species. From hatcheries come Caribbean sharp-nosed gobies, *Gobiosoma* species, together with coral gobies found in the Indo-Pacific and belonging to the genus *Gobiodon*. Gobies, like the anemonefish, dottybacks, and fairy basslets, feed mostly on plankton and adapt readily to various aquarium diets, including frozen, chopped seafood preparations and live brine shrimp nauplii.

Vegetarian fish: Vegetarian fish, such as the acanthurids, or tangs, also do well in larger coral aquariums, and will help control the growth of algae that flourishes under the illumination corals require. The Red Sea species *Zebrasoma desjardini* and the related Indo-Pacific *Z. veliferum*, both known as sailfin tang by hobbyists, are among the best. The related yellow tang, *Z. flavescens*, usually imported from Hawaii, is striking as it navigates its lemon-colored, disk-shaped body among the coral branches. Unless you have a sufficiently large aquarium to accommodate a group of three to five or more specimens, acanthurids are best maintained singly, to avoid territorial squabbles among members of the same species.

Invertebrates

Among invertebrates, perhaps the most widely maintained by coral enthusiasts are various mollusks and arthropods that feed on filamentous algae and diatoms, helping to keep these growths under control. Also prized are mollusks and echinoderms that burrow, keeping the substrate loose and aerated while feeding

on organic debris. Among the algae removers are snails in the genera *Turbo* and *Astraea*, and the hermit crabs *Clibanarius tricolor, Calcinus tibicen*, and *Paguristes cadenanti*. The hermit crabs offer the additional appeal of being brightly colored. Substrate sifters include small sea cucumbers, such as *Actinopyga* species, and serpent stars or brittlestars typified by the assortment of *Ophiocoma* and *Ophioderma* species regularly imported from the Florida Keys. Propagators offer small organisms such as these with increasing regularity, and such sources are worth investigating as a source of new discoveries for your aquarium community.

Shrimps: Several small, colorful shrimps do well in coral reef aquariums, and one, the peppermint shrimp (*Lysmata wurdemanni*), is produced through captive propagation. This species is transparent with red stripes. Red and white coloration are also found on *L. amboiensis* and *L. grabhami*, two very similar species from the Indo-Pacific and Florida, respectively, that exhibit cleaning behavior. The shrimps will alight on the body of a fish and remove parasites and dead tissue, feeding on these while performing an important service for the fish.

A few shrimps, notably several *Periclimenes* species and the pretty little *Thor amboiensis*, are regularly found living among the tentacles of corals or sea anemones. These make fascinating additions to the coral reef aquarium when the appropriate host cnidarian is available and thriving. The shrimps do no apparent harm to the host, probably feeding mostly on mucus and entrapped debris.

Much has been written about the many other reef organisms that might be included with corals in an aquarium. Consult any of the references cited in the Information section (page 91) for more detailed information than is provided in this brief summary.

Using Live Rock and Live Sand

Substrate materials taken from the ocean and shipped under conditions that permit survival of at least a portion of the invertebrates and microbes that encrust and colonize them are popular among minireef enthusiasts. Both live rock and live sand, as these materials are called, are now cultivated for the aquarium trade, although much of the supply still comes from wild harvest.

Building a Foundation

Once you have assembled the equipment and are ready to fill the aquarium with water, follow these steps to build a suitable foundation for your minireef.

1. Simply place 2 to 3 inches (5–8 cm) of sand (grain size 1–3 mm) directly on the bottom of the tank to establish the sand bed. Later, it will be inoculated with a small amount of live sand. The sand can be crushed coral, aragonite sand, or a similar product. Choose a substrate sold specifically for aquarium use. Some hobbyists like to include shell fragments and bits of coral as a small proportion of the substrate, to make it appear less monotonous.

2. Fill the tank with seawater. There should be ample water movement, although lighting can be minimal or none at this stage. Therefore, run the filtration system and any additional pumps during the "break-in" process.

3. Add enough ammonium chloride solution to give a reading of 3.0 mg/L on an ammonia

test kit. Commercial preparations of ammonium chloride (NH_4Cl) are available, or use a 6% (wt/vol) solution of reagent grade NH_4Cl in distilled water. This is added along with a few pounds of live sand as a starter.

It is likely that the pH will fall during the subsequent development of the biological filter bacteria. Maintain pH by adding limewater, enough to compensate for all evaporated water, or by using a commercial pH buffer. Sodium bicarbonate (household baking soda) can also be used as a buffer additive. A solution containing about one teaspoon (5 grams) of soda in one pint (500 ml) distilled water can be added to the tank for each 10 gallons (38 L) of water, and the resulting effect on pH noted. You can then determine how much of the

The correct (top) and incorrect (bottom) way to stack live rock.

Top: The lovely pink pigment of this
Stylophora pistillata *probably protects*
it from solar radiation.
Above: The small, colorful sea star,
Fromia, *thrives in the minireef.*
Right: The beautiful Heliofungia
actiniformis *challenges the skills*
even of experienced aquarists.

Many varieties of filter feeding invertebrates may be maintained in the minireef aquarium, including the yellow sea cucumber, Colochirus robustus.

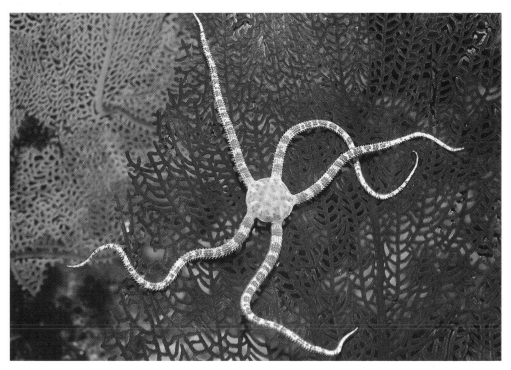

Colorful brittlestars make good additions to the minireef; this one is at home on a sea fan.

solution to add to move the pH to the desired reading. Changing the pH of the aquarium by additions of chemical should always be done slowly, so that a few tenths of a pH unit of change occurs over several days. Maintaining the pH during this phase of the aquarium's development is not crucial, but will make life easier for the aquarist later on.

4. Measure the nitrite concentration, beginning about a week after the ammonium chloride is added. Repeat the test every few days, keeping a log of the result. You should see a peak of nitrite, followed by a decline to zero. At this point, about 30 days after the live sand and ammonium chloride were first added, there will be enough nitrate in the water to be detected.

5. Begin to measure nitrate every few days. As anaerobic bacteria grow in the sand layer, the nitrate is converted to nitrogen gas, which escapes into the atmosphere. When the nitrate level is down to zero, perhaps three to four weeks later, the bacterial populations of the tank may be considered to be established and stable.

Adding Live Rock

From this point, live rock is added, the lights are turned on, and a regular maintenance routine is established. The tank will undergo a series of algal blooms for the next six to eight weeks, during which time only mobile organ-isms, and especially those that help with "housekeeping," such as snails, brittlestars, and hermit crabs, should be added. When the blooms stop, coral specimens can be added. As long as the water chemistry is maintained, the system will grow and develop from this point with little effort—apart from the maintenance duties, of course—on the aquarist's part.

Some Additional Points to Keep in Mind

1. To figure how much substrate is required, calculate the volume of the sand bed in cubic inches. One pound of live sand is about 14 cubic inches; one pound of crushed coral sand is about 18 cubic inches; one pound of aragonite, live rock fragments, or shell fragments is 23 cubic inches.

Example: Let's say we want a 2-inch (5.1 cm) layer of sand in the bottom of a 75-gallon (284 L) tank. Thus, 48" × 18" × 2" = 1,728 cubic inches. If you use all live sand, you will need 1,728/14 = 124 pounds of sand.

2. Add substrate sifters as soon as tests indicate that the development of bacterial activity in the sand bed is complete. This would be at the same time that live rock, along with algae-eating organisms, is added. The idea is to establish the community of utilitarian species that will help to maintain the environment for the more delicate species to occupy the aquarium later.

Suggested Stocking Levels, Adult Size, and Social Requirements for 24 Species of Marine Fish

Common Name	Number/ 30 gal.	Adult Size (in.)	Social Requirements
Potter's Angelfish	3	4	Solitary or harem
Pygmy Angelfish	3	2¾	Solitary or harem
Bangaii Cardinalfish	3	3	Forms shoals
Common Clownfish	3	6	Family group
Maroon Clownfish	3	7	Family group
Orange-Tailed Blue Damsel	3	3	Harem
Tomato Clownfish	3	4	Family group
Clark's Clownfish	3	4	Family group
Neon Dottyback	1	3½	Solitary or mated pair
Orchid Dottyback	1	3½	Solitary or mated pair
Mandarin Dragonet	3	4	Solitary or harem only, males fight
Royal Gramma	3	3	Solitary or harem
Blackcap Basslet	1	4	Solitary
Rainford's Goby	3	4	Solitary or group
Green-Striped Coral Goby	5	2	Solitary or group
Neon Sharp-Nosed Goby	5	2	Solitary or group
Green-Banded Goby	5	2	Solitary or group
Citron Coral Goby	5	2	Solitary or group
Long-Nosed Hawkfish	1	5	Solitary, dislikes its own kind
Flame Hawkfish	1	3	Solitary, dislikes its own kind
Yellow-Headed Jawfish	3	4	Community group
Hawaiian Lionfish	1	10	Solitary or group
Swissguard Basslet	1	3	Solitary, dislikes its own kind
Sunburst Anthias	3	3	Solitary or harem

CLASSIFICATION OF CORALS

Corals are members of the Phylum Cnidaria. All members of the phylum are animals with only two layers of cells composing the body and a single body opening. Organs are lacking, or rudimentary. Stinging cells (cnidoblasts) are present, and are a characteristic of this phylum only. Two body plans—the medusa, or jellyfish, form and the polyp, or flower-animal form— exist among cnidarians. Separation of the classes is based upon which of these two forms is predominant during the life cycle.

There are three classes of cnidarians, of which only one, Anthozoa, is covered here in depth (page 50) because it contains essentially all of the aquarium species. In general, only those anthozoan taxa containing species of aquarium interest are defined or discussed. Some groups are not discussed, but are listed only to provide a more complete picture of cnidarian diversity. Refer to Taxonomical Charts, pages 85–90, in Appendix as you read this chapter, for further information.

Class Hydrozoa

Class Hydrozoa comprises cnidarians with alternation between the two life-cycle stages,

Scientific research regularly reveals new information about corals. This one may be an undescribed species

the polyp and the medusa. Current research suggests hydrozoa evolved from the anthozoans by development of the free-swimming medusa stage.

Order Milleporina

Family Milleporidae: Only one species of hydrozoan is of potential aquarium interest, the fire coral *Millepora*. It builds a calcified skeleton, and thus is superficially similar to stony corals. *Millepora* can deliver a painful sting, and should be handled with caution. It does well in the aquarium, often obtained unintentionally as a small colony growing on a live rock specimen. Other hydrozoans, only an inch (2.5 cm) or so long, may grow upon live rock or the aquarium glass. Sometimes, such colonies produce tiny medusae that will be noticed as they swim jerkily through the aquarium.

Class Scyphozoa

Class Scyphozoa includes jellyfish or sea jellies, in which the medusa is the dominant form. This class is thought to have evolved from hydrozoans through loss of the polyp stage, which is reduced or absent in schyphozoans. Sea jellies make poor aquarium subjects, and require specially designed aquariums. They are not suitable for a community tank of corals.

Class Anthozoa

This class includes cnidarians in which the polyp form dominates the life cycle. As noted in the previous discussion, the anthozoa are thought to be the most ancient cnidarian class, having given rise to the other two.

Subclass Tabulata

The tabulate corals are all extinct, known only from fossils.

Subclass Zoantharia (=Hexacorallia)

Subclass Zoantharia is composed of solitary or colonial anthozoans with tentacles in multiples of six.

Order Zoanthidia: Order Zoanthidia consists of small anthozoans commonly called sea mats. Lacking a skeleton, sea mat polyps are usually connected by a sheet of tissue that spreads over the substrate, although some grow as individual polyps. In some cases, the colony spreads upon or throughout the body of another organism.

Indo-Pacific sea mats come in a variety of colors, including green, blue, and even pink. The Florida-Caribbean species tend to be either green or brown. Sea mats can be difficult to identify. Rocks collected with false corals (see page 59) attached may also have a sea mat colony present. These should be separated by the aquarist, as zoanthids are likely to be stung by the more aggressive false corals.

Sea mats need bright illumination, although those occurring with false corals do well under moderate light. Most rely upon photosynthesis by the zooxanthellae, but may also catch plankton. The few nonphotosynthetic sea mats depend upon planktonic food alone, which the aquarist must supply.

Suborder Brachycnemina. Family Zoanthidae: *Isaurus*, of which three species are known, is elongate, giving rise to the common name *snake polyps*. Often embedded in sand, these zoanthids prefer moderate current and bright illumination.

✔ Capable of stinging, and being stung by, other corals; allow room.

Palythoa (see photo, page 24), usually brown in color, includes species from throughout the world. Aquarists should be aware that this popular zoanthid genus produces a potent toxin, and contact should be avoided, especially if you have a cut; wear disposable latex gloves. This is an adaptable genus, and can for that reason be recommended to beginners. Provide bright light and moderate currents.

✔ Extremely toxic if eaten by fishes; may be stung by other corals.

Protopalythoa often is sold as button polyps. Colonies are usually green in color and are quite attractive. The species *P. grandis* is easily maintained under conditions of low light and moderate current.

✔ Like all zoanthids, *Protopalythoa* benefits from weekly feedings, but feeding is not necessary if lighting is sufficiently intense.

Zoanthus is a wide-ranging genus with both Atlantic and Indo-Pacific species. This genus prefers bright illumination. Many specimens are brightly colored, making it a popular genus. Look for them under the name button polyps also, often with adjectives describing the color or source of the specimens offered.

✔ All zoanthids benefit from an occasional *hurricane treatment* (see page 76) to rid them of accumulated detritus.

Suborder Macrocnemina. Family Epizoanthidae: Epizoanthids are often found in symbiotic association with other organisms. Their aquarium suitability has hardly been explored. Since they are without zooxanthellae, feeding is required.

Family Parazoanthidae: *Parazoanthus* is represented in the aquarium trade by one or more species sometimes imported from the Caribbean. Striking yellow polyps are always found embedded in the tissues of a bright red or orange sponge in an apparent symbiotic relationship. Since both the sea mat and the sponge need a constant food supply, maintaining them may prove challenging. Although these specimens are showy, they are not recommended for beginning hobbyists.
✔ Nonaggressive.

An Indo-Pacific zoantharian is known in the aquarium trade as "yellow polyp colony." Bright, lemon-yellow polyps are unusual in that they are not connected to each other, but nevertheless form closely spaced colonies on chunks of rock. Provide bright light, regular feedings, and strong current. This organism may represent an undescribed species. (See photo, page 48.)
✔ Aggressive toward many other species; allow adequate room.

Order Actinaria: Order Actinaria includes the sea anemones. These are solitary anthozoans lacking skeletal elements. Sea anemones have special needs, but sometimes do well in aquariums with corals (see my book, *Clownfishes and Sea Anemones: A Complete Pet Owner's Manual*, and other books listed on page 92 for more information on keeping sea anemones).

Order Scleractinia: Order Scleractinia includes the true or stony corals. The distinctive feature of this group is the calcified skeleton. Structural details of the skeleton serve to distinguish these anthozoans from other orders with calcified elements. Separation of species is traditionally based upon skeletal details, but recent research suggests that this may not be reliable.

Two readily distinguishable groups of scleractinian corals are seen in the aquarium trade:

1. Small-polyped scleractinian (SPS) corals are typically found on the outer reef.

2. Lagoon species, constituting the other group, have mostly large polyps, although the designation "LPS" for these species has not caught on.

Of course, stony corals can occur over a range of habitats, and many alter their growth form to take advantage of a particular microenvironment. This can make identification of species extremely difficult. Only *genera* are mentioned here, with the exception of a few species commonly seen in shops and readily identifiable.

Large-polyped stony corals are typically from shallow, relatively calm habitats, where the cone-shaped skeleton lies buried, point down, in gravel, sand, or silt. In these corals, the sexes are usually separate. Therefore, both male and female colonies must be present for fertilization to take place. Corals of this type are somewhat more tolerant of high nutrient levels, higher temperatures, and sluggish water movement than are their cousins from the outer reef.

Small-polyped scleractinian (SPS) corals reach their greatest abundance and vigor on the outer reef, where bright light, nutrient-poor conditions, and strong turbulence are the rule. Some genera also occur in the clear, quiet, shallow waters of the back reef and lagoon, where they form exceptionally beautiful, delicate colonies. In contrast to their large-polyped

Bright color forms of Acropora *are popular with hobbyists.*

Lobophyllia *is typical of corals with large polyps.*

A Caribbean species of sea mat, Zoanthus.

Palythoa vestitus, *Indo-Pacific.*

Pocillopora *is a widely available stony coral.*

Spirobranchus gigantea *extends only its feeding tentacles above the coral colony in which it lives.*

counterparts, the SPS corals typically exhibit a branching, treelike form. Many of them can be propagated simply by removing a fragment and securing it to an appropriate substrate with adhesive. Under proper care, the fragments develop into new colonies (see page 78 for more about propagating coral fragments). SPS corals are often hermaphroditic, and sexual reproduction is typically simultaneous among the majority of the species in a given geographic area, a phenomenon thought to be under the control of such factors as temperature, photoperiod, and lunar cycles.

Although it is helpful to think of corals in terms of these two basic types with differing requirements, corals are adaptable. Follow the guidelines given in the descriptions below, but

remember that the coral's growth is the best indicator that the conditions you are providing are appropriate.

Family Acroporidae. Acropora, with nearly 500 recognized species, is found in all tropical seas. Unfortunately, nearly 95 percent of the *A. palmata* and *A. cervicornis* colonies in the greater Caribbean region have been lost, due to a variety of factors, including, possibly, global warming. Aquarium *Acropora* specimens are imported from Indonesia, but good clones are available from captive propagation establishments. This genus is a good choice for beginning aquarists willing to provide bright lighting and plenty of water movement.

✔ Aggressive toward other corals, but also sensitive to the stings of some. (See photos, pages 13 [bottom] and 76.)

Family Pocilloporidae. Pocillopora, similar to *Acropora* and also having numerous species, may be easily distinguished by the lack of a terminal pore at the tip of each branchlet. *P. damicornis* (see photo, page 8 [top]) is one species that responds to propagation via fragmentation, and is widely available. Beginners should also consider this genus.

✔ Aggressive toward other corals; also sensitive to the stings of some.

Seriatopora, in particular the species *S. histrix*, is another good coral for beginners and can be obtained from propagators. This coral responds well to bright light and moderate to strong currents.

✔ Aggressive toward other corals; not particularly sensitive to the stings of other species.

Stylophora is another good choice for the beginner with an SPS tank. The species *S. pistillata* (see photo, page 44 [top]) is available from propagators. It grows well with good lighting and vigorous water movement.

✔ Aggressive toward other corals, and not particularly sensitive to the stings of other species.

Family Astrocoeniidae. This family includes only one living genus, *Stylocoeniella*, and is otherwise known only from fossils. *Stylocoeniella* is thought to be related to the pocilloporids. It is not, to my knowledge, imported for the aquarium.

Family Poritidae. Porites is a genus of many species from both the Indo-Pacific and Atlantic-Caribbean regions. Perhaps the most commonly imported species is *P. rus*, which hosts colonies of the fanworm, *Spirirobranchus gigantea*, embedded within it. Only the brightly colored appendages of the worm protrude from the surface of the coral. These worm rocks have been collected in Indonesia for the aquarium trade for many years. The coral does well, however, only under conditions of bright illumination and strong current favored by the other SPS corals mentioned in this section, and many no doubt perished before aquarists learned how to maintain them properly. These specimens are still regularly imported, but cannot be recommended to beginners. Most other species of *Porites* require more careful attention than many hobbyists are able, or willing, to provide.

✔ Aggressive toward other corals; sensitive to the stings of other species.

Goniopora, known as flowerpot coral or sunflower coral, is also difficult to maintain. A related genus, *Alveopora*, is almost indistinguishable, and is sometimes imported. Despite the fact that these genera are challenging merely to keep alive when imported from the wild, they will sometimes produce offspring—extratentacular buds—that survive and grow; therefore, some propagators are successful with this coral. Hobbyists should obtain their specimens only from such sources, and also obtain precise cultural information.

✔ In nature these corals are frequently found in large "stands" consisting of many colonies, in the absence of any other coral species.

Family Siderastreidae. Cladocora (see photo, page 8 [bottom]), is often present on cultivated live rock from the Gulf of Mexico and Florida Keys. The colonies have distinctive, star-shaped corallites visible when the polyps are withdrawn. They are typically brown in color and roughly the size of a half-dollar. They have proven hardy under a variety of aquarium conditions.

✔ Aggressive toward other corals; also sensitive to the stings of some.

Family Agariciidae. Pavona, known as lettuce coral because of its leaflike skeletal structure, is a fragile species that does not ship well, with many specimens arriving damaged. If the piece recovers from such damage, it can be expected to do best in bright light and moderate current.

✔ Aggressive toward other corals; not particularly sensitive to the stings of other species.

Family Fungiidae. A frequently imported species that beginners should avoid is *Heliofungia actiniformis*, plate coral. It needs a sandy substrate and plenty of room, because it is one of a few species capable of moving from place to place. Symbiotic shrimps, *Periclimenes holthusii* and *Thor amboiensis*, are found on this coral in nature (see photos, pages 36, 40, 44 [bottom right]). It lives in shallow water subject to intense illumination. It is difficult to keep, with mortality of aquarium specimens nearly 100 percent.

✔ Aggressive toward other corals.

Herpolitha, slipper coral or hedgehog coral, is a close relative of *Heliofungia*. Provide it with moderate light intensity and current. It should be placed on the floor of the aquarium on sand. This and a few similar corals can move about, and are likely to sustain damage if they topple from a perch upon a stack of live rock. This genus is somewhat hardier in captivity than *Heliofungia*, though not as strikingly colored.

✔ Aggressive toward other corals; also sensitive to the stings of some.

Fungia colonies are rounded disks, usually 2 to 3 inches (5–8 cm) in diameter. This common and relatively hardy member of the family is regularly available. It is adaptable to conditions of moderate lighting and current.

✔ Aggressive toward other corals; also sensitive to the stings of some.

Family Oculinidae. Galaxea often arrives in aquarium shops in damaged condition, and frequently does not recover. However, undamaged specimens adapt well to the aquarium in bright light and moderate current.

✔ Aggressive toward other corals, by means of long sweeper tentacles.

Family Pectiniidae. This small family of five genera is seldom represented in imports for the aquarium trade.

Family Mussidae. Blastomussa (see photo, page 9 [bottom]) resembles a colony of corallimorphs (see page 59). Like them, it does well in moderate to dim light and nearly calm conditions.

✔ Not aggressive toward other corals; quite sensitive to their stings.

Scolymia and *Cynarina*, both sometimes known as button coral, also consist of a single large polyp, and should receive moderate to dim illumination, with little water movement. The expanded, bubblelike structures at the margins of the skeleton add visual interest to these species.

✔ *Scolymia* is not aggressive toward other corals, but is sensitive to the stings of some. *Cynarina*, in contrast, is neither aggressive toward other corals nor particularly sensitive to their stings.

Symphyllia and *Lobophyllia* (see photo, page 52 [top right]), recognizable by the "teeth" at the margins of the colony, which are lacking in *Cynarina*, are similar in appearance otherwise, and require the same care. Place them on the bottom of a brightly illuminated aquarium, and provide only occasional water movement.

✔ Both genera are sensitive to the stings of other corals.

Above: **Galaxea,** *an oculinid stony coral found in the Indo-Pacific.*
Left: Though its large polyps are attractive, **Goniopora** *is difficult to maintain.*

Occasional feedings appear to benefit all of the corals in Family Mussidae.

Family Meandrinidae. This family consists of corals with a meandering growth pattern. They are often called brain corals. They are not, to my knowledge, seen in the aquarium trade.

Family Trachyphylliidae. Trachyphyllia geoffreyi (see photo, page 13 [top]), open brain coral, is hardy, attractive, and regularly imported. This coral is a single large polyp, a body plan that seems to be associated with ease of aquarium care. The skeleton is an inverted cone that allows the coral to sit upright in soft sand or silt. As a result of this growth form, it is

Fungia *lives on the bottom and can move about.*

It's easy to see why Cynarina lacrymalis *is known as "button coral."*

Pacifigorgia, *an Indo-Pacific sea fan, needs a constant supply of planktonic food.*

An example of Scolymia.

easily collected without damage, which may explain why aquarium specimens fare so well. *Trachyphyllia* thrives under the same conditions as those favored by false corals (see page 59).

✔ Weekly feeding enhances growth rate.

Family Faviidae. Caulastrea is easy to keep. It is known in the aquarium trade as trumpet coral, and is an attractive bright-green color. It prefers nearly calm water and strong illumination.

✔ Aggressive toward other corals; also sensitive to the stings of some.

Platygyra (see photo, page 33 [top left]) and *Leptoria*, so-called "true" brain corals, are uncommon in the trade, but both are easy to keep. In fact, all members of the Faviidae are amenable to aquarium care. Delbeek and Sprung (1994) state that bright but indirect illumination promotes the development of the most attractive colonies.

✔ Aggressive toward other corals; also sensitive to the stings of some.

Favites is often confused with a similar genus, *Favia*. Even experts have trouble distinguishing them, but this is of little concern, because care for both is the same. Provide bright indirect illumination and moderate currents. Both genera have an interesting skeleton resembling a giant honeycomb.

✔ Aggressive toward other corals; also sensitive to the stings of some.

Goniastrea is frequently found in shallow water and appreciates more light than the other species in this family. It is uncommon in the aquarium trade.

✔ Not aggressive toward other corals; sensitive to their stings.

Family Merulinidae. Hydnophora is often an appealing bright-green color, and it grows readily in bright light and good current. This is another genus that propagators can produce easily from fragments of a mother colony.

✔ Aggressive toward other corals; not particularly sensitive to the stings of other species.

Family Caryophyllidae. Catalaphyllia jardinieri, elegant coral, is one of the most popular, hardy, and spectacular corals. Like *Trachyphyllia*, it is a single polyp that lives on silt, and is easy to collect without injury. The polyps can withdraw completely into the skeleton, where they are adequately protected during transport, and the coral rarely arrives at its destination in damaged condition. This may explain why it does so well. It unfortunately often commands a premium price. Easily maintained under conditions of moderate light and enough water movement to make the tentacles sway, *Catalaphyllia* benefits from occasional feedings.

✔ Aggressive toward other corals; also sensitive to the stings of some.

Several species of *Euphyllia* are available, and all make good additions to the minireef. They have relatively long tentacles, and must not be placed close to other invertebrates, which they may sting. Provide them with bright light and enough current to move their tentacles gently. Problems with collection and transport cause many losses of these corals unnecessarily.

Euphyllia ancora—anchor coral, hammerhead coral, hammer coral, or ridge coral—has a curved extension at the end of each tentacle, giving the appearance of little hammers or anchors.

✔ Aggressive toward other corals; also sensitive to the stings of some.

Euphyllia divisa—wall coral, frogspawn coral, vase coral—gets its colorful common name from the appearance of the tentacles. It sports numerous tubercles and white spots, suggesting a mass of frog's eggs when viewed at a distance. It is another good aquarium species, although, in my experience, specimens are often lost due to shipping damage.

✔ Aggressive toward other corals; also sensitive to the stings of some.

Torch coral, *Euphyllia glabrescens*, looks like several cone-shaped torches, attached at the apex. The elongated tentacles with pale, rounded tips extend from the torchlike "flames."

✔ Aggressive toward other corals; also sensitive to the stings of some.

Plerogyra sinuosa, bubble coral, may be pale blue, brownish, or green. This is a commonly available and popular species. *Physogyra*, which looks very similar but with smaller bubbles, is called pearl bubble coral. Both bubble corals will do well in moderate light. Both also need protection from damage and produce sweeper tentacles at night.

✔ Although they produce sweeper tentacles, bubble corals may be stung by contact with other species; allow plenty of room between specimens.

Nemenzophyllia, usually known as wall coral or fox coral, has a thin skeleton constructed like a serpentine wall. The polyps, which resemble corallimorphs in their simple shape and lack of tentacles, are arrayed along the top of the wall like a row of plates along a kitchen counter. These corals from the Philippines do best with dim to moderate light and gentle water movement.

✔ Not recommended for beginners.

Family Dendrophylliidae. Turbinaria turbinata (see photo, page 25)—chalice coral, cup coral, wineglass coral—receives these common names because the skeleton is shaped like a goblet with a fat stem by which the coral is attached to a hard substrate. Thin brownish tissue covers the entire surface, so it is important to avoid specimens that have merely been snapped off above the point of attachment. The large, flowerlike polyps are borne only on the inside of the "goblet." *T. turbinata* is interesting in appearance, and easy to keep. Other species of *Turbinaria* are thinner and more delicate in appearance, and are good aquarium subjects as well. Often, such specimens are an attractive mustard-yellow color. Moderate to bright light and moderate currents suit this coral best.

✔ Aggressive toward other corals; also sensitive to the stings of some.

Tubastrea is one of the genera that lack zooxanthellae. Its requirement for regular feedings makes it rather difficult to keep, although aquarists seldom fail to be attracted by its brilliant orange coloration and large polyps. Given enough food, the coral grows slowly under captive conditions. Larvae of this species have established themselves in the aquarium after being released from a gravid individual fertilized in the wild. Nevertheless, *Tubastrea* cannot be recommended for beginners. It requires dim light, but good current, and daily feedings.

✔ Probably not aggressive toward zooxanthellate corals, since it does not share habitat with them; may be stung by other corals.

Order Corallimorpharia: Order Corallimorpharia is composed of the *false corals*. They are usually colonial and lack a skeleton. Most of these anthozoans are flat, rounded polyps with short columns. Tentacles are completely lacking in some species, while in others the presence of

Trachyphyllia geoffroyi, *typical color form.*

Leptoria, *one of several "brain" corals.*

Caulastrea *can be propagated from fragments.*

Favites, *showing the characteristic "honeycomb" arrangement of the corallites.*

Astraea *snails help keep the aquarium free of algae.*

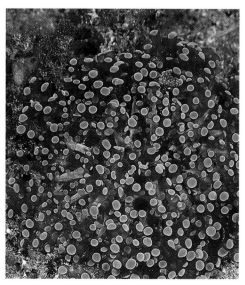

The polyps of Euphyllia divisa *resemble a mass of frog's eggs.*

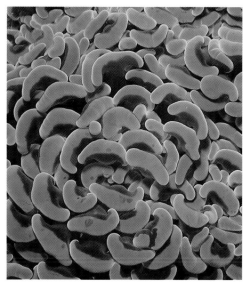

Euphyllia ancora, *with its hammerhead polyps, is hardy in the aquarium.*

Euphyllia glabrescens, *another popular and commonly available caryophyllid.*

numerous short tentacles results in their being called "fuzzy" by dealers.

Also called disc anemones, mushroom corals, and corallimorphs, false corals are usually blue-green, brown, or green. Some have blue or red pigments, and are thus especially attractive aquarium specimens. The false corals of interest to aquarists all possess zooxanthellae, but typically do well in moderate to low levels of light. They can be placed near the bottom of the aquarium, where lighting is reduced, if maintained in the same tank with light-loving species. Any species is a good choice for a coral community aquarium, although they are often aggressive, stinging other corals that make contact. One, *Amplexidiscus*, is capable of catching fish, but most others rely entirely on photosynthesis, or supplement photosynthesis with plankton.

Generally easy to maintain, false corals often multiply with no encouragement from the aquarist. They are readily available from propagators, and can be recommended to the beginner without reservation, thriving in tanks with simple lighting and filtration. The taxonomy of this group has been in disarray, and many species names that one sees applied in the literature are probably synonyms. Similarly, the names assigned below will be disagreed upon by some experts.

Family Sideractidae. To my knowledge, sideractids are seldom, if ever, imported for aquariums.

Family Corallimorphidae. Both temperate and tropical false corals, such as *Corynactis*, *Pseudocorynactis*, and *Corallimorphus*, are assigned to this family. They are uncommon in the aquarium trade.

Family Discosomatidae. *Discosoma*, of which four species are probably in the aquarium trade, is the most widely available false coral. Its polyps are simple round disks, attached in clusters to a solid surface. Individual polyps may reproduce by budding off small fragments from the body margin. These float away and subsequently grow into new polyps. Highly variable, the organism can range from brown to blue or red, and the disk may be decorated with various spots and stripes in contrasting pale green. *Discosoma* grows easily in indirect light, with nearly calm conditions.

✔ Aggressive toward stony corals, but may also be stung by them; allow room between specimens.

Paradiscosoma calgreni is commonly called the "neon disc anemone." It is collected in the Caribbean, and is as hardy and adaptable as the other corallimorphs. Provide moderate light and little water movement.

✔ Although small in size, it is aggressive toward other species.

Rhodactis, represented in the trade by several species, has obvious tufted or bubblelike tentacles, but otherwise is as variable as *Discosoma*. It requires the same care and can be cultivated alongside *Discosoma* in the aquarium. Perhaps the most sought-after form of this genus is the one known in the trade as Tongan blue mushroom polyp because of its coloration.

✔ Aggressive toward stony corals, but is stung by some; allow room.

Amplexidiscus, or elephant ear false coral, is perhaps the largest corallimorph species, reaching nearly a foot (30 cm) across. It has a propensity to eat small fish that may be unwary of its stubby tentacles, but makes a spectacular specimen if given sufficient room to expand without touching neighboring invertebrates. There is a single species, *A. fenestrafer*, in the aquarium trade. It is zooxanthellate, adapting well to various light regimes. It prefers calm to moderate current.

✔ Aggressive toward stony corals and fish.

Family Ricordeidae. Ricordea includes two species, one found in the tropical Atlantic-Caribbean region, and the other in the Indo-Pacific. Collection of the former, *R. florida*, is restricted, and specimens are therefore not as readily available to aquarists as they once were. It multiplies slowly, but is nevertheless produced commercially by propagators. Long a favorite of aquarists, the polyps are round disks studded with tentacles like beads about 2 mm in diameter, in neon green or orange, and sometimes pink or blue coloration. This genus is not recommended for beginners, although it grows in indirect light and moderate to calm current.

✔ Like other corallimorphs, *Ricordea* should be prevented from contacting other species.

Order Ceriantipatharia: Order Ceriantipatharia includes the tube anemones and black corals, characterized by having two kinds of tentacles. Both types of ceriantipatharians have specialized cultural needs, and are not appropriate for the minireef aquarium. Black corals are prized for their skeletons, used in jewelry making.

Order Rugosa: The rugose corals are an extinct group of hexacorals.

Subclass Octocorallia

Anthozoans that possess tentacles in multiples of eight are included in this subclass. All are colonial. They are usually known as *soft corals*. Photosynthetic soft corals are enormously popular aquarium subjects. For one thing, they are amenable to propagation by

simple asexual reproduction, so hobbyists can increase their stock rather easily. Nonphotosynthetic species, while more challenging to keep because of their need for regular feedings with a plankton substitute, are nevertheless often attempted by aquarists because of their beautiful coloration.

Many other families and subfamilies of soft corals are recognized by biologists, but few are represented in the aquarium trade. None of these species are discussed here.

Order Helioporacea (=Coenothecalia): The Order Helioporacea (Coenothecalia) includes two families, Lithotelestidae and Helioporidae.

Family Helioporidae. Order Helioporacea has but one representative in the tropics, *Heliopora*, which was once widely collected for its blue skeleton as a curio. The living animal is a dull-brown color and not widely sought after as an aquarium subject. Where individual polyps emerge from the skeletal mass, their cups are not divided into segments by spokelike septa, as are the cups of scleractinian corals.

Order Alcyonacea: Soft corals in which the skeleton is made up of loose elements constitute this order. Included species are among the most popular soft corals for aquarium culture. Alcyonacea is divided into two suborders, Protoalcyonaria and Stolonifera.

Suborder Stolonifera. Suborder Stolonifera includes octocorals in which the polyps in some species are connected by tubes of tissue that resemble the runners, or stolons, found on plants such as strawberries. In other species, the connections appear more like sheets of tissue.

Within this suborder, there exists the Family Clavulariidae, which contains the Subfamily Clavulariinae.

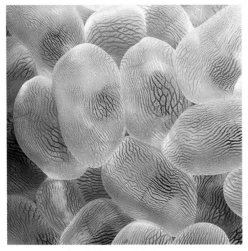

Close-up of bubble coral, Plerogyra sinuosa.

Despite being difficult, Tubastrea *attracts aquarists with its bright coloration.*

Left: Plexaura, *shown here with expanded polyps, is typical of the photosynthetic gorgonians found in the Caribbean. Above: Of limited distribution,* Catalaphyllia jardinieri *is costly, but popular with hobbyists.*

A blue Discosoma *from the Indo-Pacific.*

Florida false coral, Ricordea florida.

Paradiscosoma calgreni *from the Caribbean.*

Tubipora musica, *a stoloniferan soft coral.*

Clavularia forms matlike colonies with the brown, star-shaped polyps rising 1 centimeter (0.4 inch) or so above the surface. This soft coral spreads rapidly under appropriate conditions of strong light and moderate current. It goes by the common name of clove polyps.

✔ Not aggressive toward other corals; may overgrow them.

Another family within the Suborder Stolonifera is Tubiporidae. *Tubipora musica*, organ pipe coral, possesses a wine-colored skeleton that is heavily calcified and shows distinct layering. The starlike polyps are similar in appearance to those of *Briareum* (see page 70). This organism is a good example of one that possesses a calcified skeleton but is not a scleractinian. Best results in growing this species are obtained in bright light and varying currents.

✔ Damaged specimens may not recover. Not recommended for beginners.

Pachyclavularia is discussed with *Briareum*, on page 70. It is sometimes assigned to the Tubiporidae.

Suborder Alcyoniina. A second suborder within Alcyonacea is Alcyoniina. Many members of Suborder Alcyoniina are important to aquarium hobbyists, owing to the ease with which they can be propagated, although some are unusually demanding in their requirements.

In the leather corals, as many of these soft corals are commonly known, the body is typically brownish or yellowish in color, and the polyps are embedded in it. Leather corals generally prefer high light intensities, as they often grow in shallow water. They need a stable pH, around 8.3 to 8.4. Such conditions are also favored by many green macroalgae, nicely contrasting with the brown to yellow-brown color of the corals, so it is not uncommon to find aquarists growing them together with visually impressive results. The polyps of leather corals may remain withdrawn for several days after a sudden change in water conditions (such as being moved from one aquarium to the other). After they recover from the change, normal, healthy leather corals usually have their polyps expanded toward the light, and slowly grow to form robust specimens.

Within Alcyoniina is the Family Alcyoniidae. *Sarcophyton* (see photo, page 84), a genus with many species, is usually called leather mushroom soft coral, or something similar, by aquarium dealers. The colony is shaped like a toadstool, with the polyps protruding from pores on the cap. It is one of the most widely available and hardy genera among the entire group. It grows in turbid water and appreciates moderate light and current. An occasional strong current surge helps to dislodge debris that may accumulate on the cap.

✔ A good choice for beginners.

Lobophytum (see photo, page 28), often called devil's hand soft coral, has only a few short polyps protruding from a skeleton shaped roughly like an outstretched hand. It is tolerant of a wide range of conditions in the aquarium, and is therefore a good choice for the novice aquarist.

✔ Aggressive toward other corals through its chemical secretions. Unfortunately, species that react negatively to its presence in the tank must be moved to other quarters.

Alcyonium is sometimes sold as "colt coral." The colony consists of soft, flowing branches, usually in brown or yellowish hues. It grows easily, spreading under bright light and strong current when established in the aquarium.

Obtain specimens from propagators, since recently collected individuals need time to adapt.

✔ Aggressive toward other corals by overgrowing them. Prune appropriately, and use the pieces to start new colonies.

Sinularia, lettuce or cauliflower soft coral, possesses large skeletal elements. Provide bright, indirect light and moderate to strong water movement.

✔ Easily propagated and recommended for beginners.

Another family contained in Suborder Alcyoniina is Nephtheidae. *Dendronephthya* (see photo, page 32) is known by a variety of trade names, referring usually to its lovely pink or orange coloration. With a delicate appearance resembling blown art glass, the translucent tissues are flecked with embedded skeletal elements. This soft coral requires daily feedings with cultured unicellular algae, and is likely to thrive only in the hands of a dedicated and experienced aquarist.

✔ Not recommended.

Scleronephthya is much like the preceding genus. Although lovely, this coral requires a lot of work to maintain. Leave it to the professionals unless you are prepared to provide the appropriate food organisms on a regular basis.

✔ Not recommended.

Lemnalia is called tree coral, a name that adequately describes the form of the light brown colonies. It appreciates strong lighting, but adapts to lower light levels with correspondingly slow growth. Strong turbulence periodically and moderate current otherwise appear to suit it best.

✔ Easily propagated; recommended for beginners.

Also contained with this suborder is the Family Xeniidae. Several species of these soft corals are interesting because they exhibit rhythmic pulsing movements. These are collectively referred to as *pulse corals*. All can be recommended for the beginning enthusiast, and can be obtained from captive-propagated sources. The aquarium species reproduce readily from cuttings. Not all species in these genera exhibit pumping movements, but the motionless ones are nevertheless worth growing. Provide strong lighting and adjust the current so that the polyps are washed by it gently, but not intimidated into cessation of their movements. Getting it just right can be a matter of trial and error.

Xenia (see photo, page 16), characterized by individual polyps that are long and thin, reminds one of a daisy. Most species are a pale bluish-brown color. Grow *Xenia* under bright light, with varying current.

✔ Easily propagated; recommended for beginners.

Anthelia sports feathery white polyps attached at the base to form a cluster anchored to a rock. It needs strong light and more vigorous current than does *Xenia*.

✔ Easily propagated; recommended for beginners.

Heteroxenia specimens may stop pumping when currents, which transport nutrients to it and carry away its wastes, are too vigorous. It does not possess nematocysts, and probably relies exclusively on photosynthesis for nourishment—therefore its need for bright illumination. As is the case with *Xenia*, variation in the direction and force of water movement appears to be beneficial.

*Above: The giant false coral, **Amplexidiscus fenestrafer**, showing both expanded and closed polyps.*

Opposite page:
*Top left: **Sarcophyton** colonies often are shaped like a toadstool.*
*Top right: Captured as the polyps close in unison, this pulse coral, **Xenia**, lives in Papua-New Guinea.*
*Bottom left: **Sinularia**, photographed in the Maldives.*
*Bottom right: **Anthelia** colonies are often an attractive pale blue color.*

✔ Capable of rapid growth that can smother other corals; thus an ideal choice for captive propagation.

Cespitularia produces rather unusual colonies that are sometimes bright blue in color. It demands bright light and strong current. This genus is more difficult to culture than the others in its family.
✔ Not recommended.

Some of the remaining octocorals, or gorgonians, are commonly known as sea whips or sea fans, because of their body structure. Still others of this group are flattened, encrusting forms. The skeleton in all of them is composed of the protein gorgonin and calcareous spicules.

The arrangement of the skeletal elements is important in classification. Sea fans are distinctive in that the branches are fused to form a net. Surrounding the axial skeleton is the living coral colony, often brilliantly colored.

Shallow water gorgonians are usually photosynthetic, while their deep-water counterparts normally depend upon catching plankton for food. These differences must be borne in mind when caring for them. Gorgonians are divided into two groups, based upon the structure of the axial skeleton.

Suborder Scleraxonia. This is another suborder contained in the Order Alcyonacea, and comprises a number of different families and their associated subfamilies.

One such family is Briareidae. Green starburst soft coral, *Briareum viridis* (see photo, page 33 [bottom]), is also called green star polyps, and is frequently misidentified as *Tubipora musica*, a stoloniferan. There is considerable confusion about the precise taxonomic status of this soft coral, with some authors assigning it to the Tubiporidae and to the genus *Pachyclavularia*. I retain here the older classification within the suborder Scleraxonia. The skeleton is a rubbery, flattened sheet, usually purplish in color, that encrusts a solid substrate. Each polyp resides in a short tube that projects upward from the basal sheet about a centimeter. The polyps are often pale green with contrasting bright-green centers, or may be lime-green entirely. When expanded, this is a beautiful species. It is also, happily, one of the hardiest and most durable of organisms, and can be recommended even to the beginner. Its only requirements seem to be moderate current and bright light, under which conditions it will grow and spread.

✔ Highly recommended, although it may overgrow and kill stony corals.

Another family, Anthothelidae, contains the subfamily Spongiodermatinae. *Erythropodium* greatly resembles *Briareum*. It spreads its pinkish skeleton over solid objects in shallow inshore waters, where it receives maximum solar exposure and variable current. The golden-brown polyps are large and elongate, and flutter with the movements of the water.

✔ Easy and recommended for beginners.

The Family Corallidae is another member of Suborder Scleraxonia. Although not imported for the aquarium, the genus *Corallium* may be familiar as the precious coral used in jewelry.

Suborder Holaxonia. Holaxonia is another suborder within the Order Alcyonacea. It, too, comprises a number of families and their related subfamilies.

One such family is Plexauridae. The Subfamily Plexaurinae is one of two subfamilies contained within Plexauridae. *Eunicea* is called knobby candelabrum, adequately describing its appearance. It lives on hard substrates in shallow water, exposed to bright light and strong tidal surges. Feed it several times a week, even though it possesses zooxanthellae.

✔ Recommended for a shallow-water habitat tank.

Muricea, or spiny sea whip, can easily be recognized by the sharp projections of the axial skeleton, which are evident when handled. Care is similar to that of the preceding genus, and indeed is similar for all of the zooxanthellate gorgonians.

✔ Produces sweeper tentacles; provide adequate spacing.

Muriceopsis is known as sea plume because the rounded branches of the axial skeleton are oppositely arranged, resembling a feather. Requirements for this genus are the same as for those above.

✔ Produces sweeper tentacles; provide adequate spacing.

Plexaura is often called sea rod, a reference to the rounded branches, which are as thick as a human pinky finger. Care for this genus is similar to that of others, but the genus cannot be recommended, since specimens apparently do not ship well and most fail to adapt to the aquarium.

✔ Not recommended.

The second subfamily, Stenogorgiinae, contains *Swiftia*. *Swiftia* is the orange tree gorgonian collected in the Caribbean. With red polyps protruding from a bright orange axial skeleton, this is among the most attractive sea whips. Unfortunately, it is difficult to keep. (See photo, page 93.)

✔ Not recommended, as it requires frequent feedings.

Gorgoniidae is another family within the Suborder Holaxonia and contains *Gorgonia*. *Gorgonia* is a genus of several species in the Caribbean, all known as sea fans because their branches are fused together, forming a roughly triangular net that can reach 1 meter in height. Specimens much smaller than this are suitable for an aquarium with moderate to bright illumination and moderate water movement. (See photo, page 12 [bottom].)

✔ Sprung and Delbeek (see Information, page 91) mention that sea fans prefer water movement that rocks them to and fro.

Pacifigorgia is the Indo-Pacific equivalent of the Caribbean sea fans, but the genus lacks zooxanthellae. Therefore, though colorful, it should be avoided by beginners because of its requirement for copious feeding. (See photo, page 57 [bottom left].)

✔ Not recommended.

Pseudopterogorgia is one of the *sea feathers*, with the branches arising in a single plane, somewhat resembling an ostrich plume. It is often a rich purple color and needs bright light and good water movement. Orient the flow so that the gorgonian's body plane is perpendicular to the current.

✔ Among the best choices for the aquarium.

Pterogorgia, another sea feather, is also hardy. Give it the same conditions as described above for other zooxanthellate gorgonians. Although collected in the Caribbean, it grows easily, and can be propagated from cuttings.

✔ Suitable for beginners.

Order Pennatulacea: Pennutulacea is the third order contained in the Subclass Octocorallia. Order Pennatulacea includes the sea pens. They live partially buried in a soft substrate, extending a portion of the colony into the water to capture plankton. Some are bioluminescent. Sea pens are not often seen in the aquarium trade, and must have aquariums designed to conform to their peculiar requirements.

Besides maintaining the various important physical and chemical properties of the water, as discussed beginning on page 18, the minireef aquarium requires regular and consistent attention to keep the corals and their tankmates thriving. At most, this will require about an hour a week of concentrated effort, with a major cleaning about once a month. Most of the work will be changing water, which every aquarist seems to hate, but that nevertheless must be done sooner or later. As with many chores, regular, small adjustments are less time and energy consuming than a major overhaul.

The primary criterion of the success of aquarium maintenance procedures is the growth of the corals. If they are thriving, your technique is good; if not, then you should look for the source of the problem and correct it immediately. Beginners are often advised to observe healthy corals in public aquarium exhibits and in the homes of accomplished aquarist friends, as well as to examine the photographs in books such as this. These are excellent ways to learn how your specimens should look.

Shallow water corals often grow alongside seaweeds that can also be exhibited in the aquarium.

Routine Aquarium Maintenance

Seawater confined in an aquarium is subject to fluctuations in chemical and physical parameters and accumulation of wastes. Therefore, the most important aspect of maintaining a minireef aquarium is keeping environmental conditions within rather narrow limits. This is easily accomplished by making regular observations and tests, and then carrying out appropriate adjustments. For example, the aquarium's temperature can rise or fall with changing conditions in the room where the aquarium is kept. Adjustments might thus involve something as simple as resetting a thermostat to keep the temperature of the aquarium constant despite those fluctuations. Evaporation will cause a gradual, but significant, increase in salinity, as the same quantity of salts is concentrated in a smaller volume of water. Phosphate and other nutrient compounds may accumulate to many times their natural levels, resulting in a bloom of algae growth. It is the aquarist's job to ensure that the magnitude of these inevitable changes in conditions is minimized through appropriate maintenance.

Most of the time, this means testing the water regularly and making appropriate adjustments when conditions begin to deviate from their target values to a minor degree. Remember, "Test, then tweak," is the rule of thumb. Neglecting maintenance to the point that major perturbations must be corrected with a massive water change—to mention one common mistake—is a near guarantee of major problems with the organisms inhabiting the tank.

Specific information about the chemical tests one should perform, and recommendations for making adjustments, are found on page 34.

Water Changes

Some hobbyists find that changing some water on a regular basis is the best way to maintain water quality. Others change water only when tests indicate that too many nutrients are accumulating. Regardless of the approach you ultimately choose as the best one for your aquarium, sooner or later you will need to replace some seawater; therefore, making and storing synthetic seawater is a basic skill.

Seawater: Aquarists who have convenient access to natural seawater should use it. Some hobbyists elect to disinfect freshly collected seawater by adding chlorine and then removing the chlorine with a commercial dechlorinator. Others simply allow the water to stand, covered, in a cool, dark place for a week or so. In some large coastal cities, seawater can be purchased from service companies that collect, disinfect, and deliver the water to your door. For the majority of hobbyists, however, synthetic seawater, made up using dry salt mix and fresh water, is the most satisfactory way to obtain this essential component of any marine aquarium.

Regardless of the source, replacement seawater must be similar to the water in the tank in terms of its temperature, specific gravity, and pH before you add it to the aquarium.

If stored covered in a cool, dark place such as a garage, basement, or closet, seawater remains suitable for aquarium use almost indefinitely, so it is easy to mix up a large amount to have available for water changes as needed. A covered plastic container is ideal for storing seawater. Five-gallon (19 L) plastic pails used for jelly or pastry cream can sometimes be obtained free from food service companies and bakeries.

Tap water: Aquarists do not often give any thought to the quality of the fresh water that they use to prepare synthetic seawater, and most use plain tap water. I recommend strongly against this, as, unfortunately, municipal tap water and well water are frequently unsatisfactory for aquarium use. This is due to the presence of pollutants that, while perhaps not considered harmful for drinking purposes, can cause problems in the marine aquarium. Nutrients such as phosphate and silica, toxic metals such as copper, and a host of other compounds may all be found in tap water (see page 17 for a discussion of water purification via reverse osmosis).

Salinity: A little more than two cups of dry seawater mix will make 5 gallons (19 L) of seawater. Start with this ratio, but make final adjustments based on salinity measurement. Buy dry salt mix in large quantities to save on its cost. It keeps indefinitely if stored in a tightly sealed container away from moisture, which promotes caking.

Temperature: A common problem with stored seawater is that the storage temperature is cooler than the temperature of the tank. Here are two tips for solving this problem:

1. Make a concentrated brine by dissolving the required amount of salt in only two-thirds as much water as you are going to need. When ready to use, add heated fresh water to the brine to dilute it to the correct specific gravity.

2. Or prepare water to the desired specific gravity and store it. When ready to use, heat a portion of the water to the temperature of a cup of coffee, using your microwave oven, and mix the heated water back into the cooler water to raise its temperature to that of the tank.

Note: Never heat seawater to the boiling point, and never heat it in a metal container.

Feeding

Feeding is another important aspect of maintaining a minireef aquarium. In a well-established system, there will be an abundance of small organisms—microcrustaceans and algae, for example—that serve as food for invertebrates and fish. While these foods are excellent sources of nourishment for captive specimens, they often cannot be relied upon as an exclusive food source, because they may not be produced in sufficient amounts in the confines of the aquarium.

While virtually all anthozoans feed by capturing plankton with their tentacles, photosynthesis by their zooxanthellae provides sufficient nourishment for many to grow and reproduce without added foods. On the other hand, many hobbyists report increased growth by corals that are fed regularly. Anthozoans that lack zooxanthellae must be fed regularly, perhaps the chief reason that these species are more difficult to maintain than those bearing the symbionts.

For a newly established minireef with zooxanthellate anthozoans and no fish, it is probably best not to add food until the system has been running for about six weeks or more, since new systems are unstable, often undergoing successive blooms of algae, for example. Adding additional nutrients is counterproductive. One sign that the system is maturing properly is the replacement of fast-growing filamentous algae with encrusting, purple coralline algae. At that point, you might add a small amount of a suitable plankton substitute, such as live brine shrimp nauplii or cultured unicellular algae, several times a week, noting the effects on water chemistry and the condition of the corals. In this way, you can gradually develop an appropriate feeding regimen for the particular community you have assembled. Increased growth of the corals with no change in the system's "nitrogen budget" (see page 22) indicates success in this regard.

Amount to Feed

Fish that are included in the minireef, on the other hand, should be fed once or twice daily, in small portions. Added fish foods are a major source of nutrient ions, and the concentration of these substances in the water must be kept to a minimum. The food supply should be adjusted so that fish consume as much of the food as possible, and little sinks to the bottom to decay. Deciding how much to give at a feeding will take some experimentation on the part of the aquarist, as each community of fish is different. Never mind that the fish always seem hungry when you approach the tank—the fact that they are willing to eat does not mean that they should be fed. Establish a regular feeding schedule and stick to it. Monitor the effects on accumulation of nitrate, scheduling water changes to compensate for this buildup.

Cleaning

Algae growing on the tank glass should be removed when it becomes unsightly. Follow these measures:

1. Use a scouring pad made for nonstick cookware to wipe off stubborn growths, or buy one of the various devices sold for the purpose at aquarium shops.

2. Clean accumulated salts from the aquarium cover by rinsing with tap water. Water splattering on the underside of the cover glass supports the growth of algae and leaves mineral deposits. To clean, remove the cover and apply vinegar to the mineral deposits, which should come off easily after soaking a few moments.

3. Clean the exterior of the aquarium only with products made specifically for the purpose, or with plain water only. Polish with a clean, dry cloth. Tanks made of acrylic scratch easily; therefore, care must be taken when cleaning one, inside or out, to avoid trapping grit between the cloth and the tank, thus marring the surface.

4. Accumulated material from the protein skimmer must be emptied as it collects. About once a month, the skimmer should be disman-tled for a thorough cleaning to remove the film that develops on the inside, reducing skimming efficiency.

5. Debris accumulation should be periodically reduced by siphoning, perhaps once every week or two.

6. Twice a year, one can simulate the effects of a hurricane by using a powerhead held in the hand to direct a strong jet of water on, around, and between the rocks constituting the minireef. This will stir up a large amount of debris. Running an extra canister filter on the tank for a day or two afterward will pick up much loose material, or one can simply do a large water change, siphoning off as much suspended matter as possible.

Acropora is only one of many stony corals that can be propagated from cuttings.

Reddish-brown flatworms infest this **Cynarina** *coral.*

Predators, such as this sea slug, often closely resemble the corals upon which they feed.

Pests

Despite your best efforts at husbandry, pests and pathogens will eventually find their way into the aquarium. Usually, such invasions are no cause for panic, and certainly do not call for the drastic measures that some aquarists take. Many coral parasites are opportunists that attack corals weakened by poor environmental conditions; therefore, care in maintaining a proper environment will do more toward keeping corals healthy than adding chemical treatments to the tank.

Aquarists who keep fish are more likely to have parasite problems with them than with corals, judging from the experiences of many hobbyists. Treatment for the most common fish parasites is straightforward, but absolutely must take place in an aquarium other than the coral tank. Consult references listed in the Information (page 91) for treatment procedures. Fortunately, aquarists report that fish maintained in minireef systems have fewer problems with parasites than do those in fish-only aquarium displays.

Having a separate aquarium can be quite useful in the treatment of problems with corals, also. It should have moderate water movement, a protein skimmer, and sufficient illumination. Usually, such a tank is employed to isolate new specimens, to treat ailing specimens, and to allow the recovery of a specimen after treatment.

Hobbyists sometimes complain about the cost of establishing a second aquarium, particularly a "hospital" not on display for family and friends. However, the investment in a spare tank is usually fairly small in comparison to the cost of specimens spared from the trash bin by using one. For more on pests, see Dealing with Some Common Problems, page 79.

Propagation

Propagating corals can add much to the hobbyist's enjoyment of a minireef. The references included in the Information (see page 91) contain detailed explanations of how to go about propagating various species, but the basic techniques are simple. A fragment of the coral colony is removed and affixed to a base where it eventually grows into a new colony.

Soft corals are among the easiest to propagate from cuttings. Using a razor blade, take a cutting from the margin of the colony. Place the cutting between two small rocks held together by a rubber band. The band should provide enough pressure to hold the cutting in place without crushing it. After several weeks, it will have grown securely to the rocks and the rubber band can be removed. Nylon fishing line can also be used to secure cuttings.

Cuttings may be propagated from stony corals in a similar way, except that a sturdier implement is needed to remove a fragment from the colony. A pair of electricians' wire cutters works well. Products such as underwater epoxy and cyanoacrylate glue are used to attach the fragments to a base. Branching stony corals, in particular, are amenable to this procedure. In the case of corals that consist of a single large polyp, the colonies may simply be broken in two using a hammer and chisel. Many, in fact, are collected from the reef in this way. Some corals produce "baby" colonies at the base of the parent colony without intervention from the aquarist.

For many species, the coral can simply be allowed to grow on a rock placed in close proximity. Once well established, the colony on the rock can be separated from the original. This works well for soft corals, such as *Briareum* and *Xenia*.

False corals produce new colonies by budding. Gently scraping a small polyp from its rock and repositioning it elsewhere is a simple and effective means of propagation.

Some hobbyists have found that they can sell coral colonies to their local aquarium dealer. One organization, Geothermal Aquaculture Research Foundation, even offers seminars that teach coral propagation. According to the organization's founder, some of its students have gone on to start successful businesses. Most hobbyists, however, are content to trade coral fragments with fellow hobbyists, or simply use their home-grown corals to start new minireefs.

Dealing with Some Common Problems

Brown jelly: Corals weakened by injury or poor environmental conditions may be attacked by pathogens and parasites. Ciliated protozoans are responsible for the problem known as *brown jelly* that may develop at the margin of an injury. Brown jelly can be controlled on stony corals by carefully siphoning off the jelly and loose, dead tissue and then submerging the coral in a bath of freshwater at the same temperature as the aquarium for about five minutes. Return the coral to the display aquarium, or preferably to a separate recovery tank with appropriate environmental conditions. Soft corals with brown jelly should have the injured area carefully cleaned in seawater, and the infected tissue excised with a sharp instrument.

Flatworms: Flatworms that prey on corals are sometimes imported along with a specimen. A brief freshwater bath may cause them to release their hold, so many hobbyists routinely treat new stony corals this way. Inspect new specimens carefully, especially for the first few days after placing them in the aquarium. Often, one or two flatworms can simply be removed with forceps before they multiply into a plague. This is the best method for false corals, sea mats, soft corals and similar specimens that do not respond well to a freshwater dip.

Mollusks: Certain mollusks, particularly sea slugs, may feed exclusively on one or a few types of corals. These pests may be difficult to detect because they often closely resemble their prey. Try inspecting corals after dark with a flashlight. Sea slugs are usually brought into the aquarium along with their prey species—such as a soft coral colony—and seldom stray far from it.

Aiptasia anemones: These may become a pest in aquariums with bright illumination and abundant nutrients. These pale, brown anemones seldom reach more than 3 inches (7.6 cm) in height. They find their way into the aquarium on rocks. They multiply readily and their stings can adversely affect corals. Take care to remove any individuals you notice. Once the aquarium becomes overrun, eradication of these pests can be difficult. The copperband butterflyfish, *Chelmon rostratus*, is effective in controlling *Aiptasia*, and although it may nibble at corals occasionally, it normally does little harm.

Algae: One other problem may be the encroachment of algae. The best approach to dealing with this is the inclusion of herbivores in the aquarium and keeping nutrient levels, particularly phosphate, as low as possible.

APPENDIX

Coral Anatomy and Terminology

Marine biologists use a lexicon of specialized terminology for describing corals. Understanding this terminology makes it possible for the novice to use more advanced references on the identification of coral species. The most important terms are identified in the accompanying illustration on page 83.

Marine Aquarium Water Quality Parameters

Marine environments are extremely stable, particularly where corals live. Significant deviation outside the range given for any of the parameters may lead to problems in the aquarium.

✔ Temperature— 74°–82°F (23°–28°C)
✔ Salinity—34–36 ppt
✔ pH—8.15–8.6 (8.2–8.3 optimum)
✔ Alkalinity—2.0–5. 0 meq/L (6–15 dKH)
✔ Ammonia (NH_3)—Zero
✔ Nitrite (NO_2^-)—Zero
✔ Nitrate (NO_3^-)—< 20 mg/L (as nitrate ion)
✔ Nitrate (NO_3^-)—<4.55 mg/L (as nitrate-nitrogen)

✔ Phosphate (PO_4^{3-})—<0.05 mg/L
✔ Calcium (Ca^{2+})—375–475 mg/L
✔ Dissolved Oxygen (O_2)—> 6.90 mg/L

Salinity Determination from Hydrometer Readings

When the specific gravity of aquarium water is measured with a hydrometer, the salinity of the water can be calculated if the temperature is also known.

First, convert the temperature reading to Celsius, by using the following formula:

$$°C = 0.56 \, (°F - 32)$$

Next, read across to find the temperature in Table 1, and then read down in that column to the row corresponding to the hydrometer reading. The number in the table is a conversion factor, which should be added to the hydrometer reading. Two leading zeros are assumed. The result is the density of the water.

Finally, using Table 2, look up the salinity that corresponds to the density you just calculated.

Brilliantly colored soft corals decorate a reef in the Red Sea.

Table 1: Conversion of Specific Gravity Readings to Density

Observed Hydrometer Reading	Temperature (°C)						
	20°	21°	22°	23°	24°	25°	26°
1.0170	10	12	15	17	20	22	25
1.0180	10	12	15	17	20	23	25
1.0190	10	12	15	18	20	23	26
1.0200	10	13	15	18	20	23	26
1.0210	10	13	15	18	21	23	26
1.0220	11	13	15	18	21	23	26
1.0230	11	13	16	18	21	24	26
1.0240	11	13	16	18	21	24	27
1.0250	11	13	16	18	21	24	27
1.0260	11	13	16	19	22	24	27
1.0270	11	14	16	19	22	24	27
1.0280	11	14	16	19	22	25	28
1.0290	11	14	16	19	22		

Table 2: Conversion of Density to Salinity

Density	Salinity	Density	Salinity	Density	Salinity
1.0180	25	1.0225	30	1.0270	36
1.0185	25	1.0230	31	1.0275	37
1.0190	26	1.0235	32	1.0280	38
1.0195	27	1.0240	32	1.0285	38
1.0200	27	1.0245	33	1.0290	39
1.0205	28	1.0250	34	1.0295	40
1.0210	29	1.0255	34	1.0300	40
1.0215	29	1.0260	35		
1.0220	30	1.0265	36		

Natural salinity is 35 in the vicinity of most coral reefs, unless the ocean is diluted from a nearby freshwater source. The acceptable range for invertebrates is 34 to 36, while fishes can tolerate lower salinities.

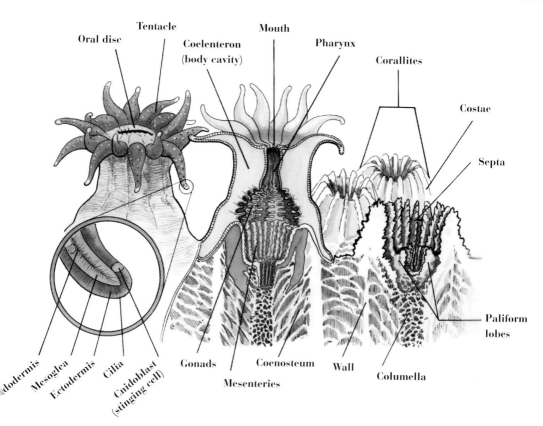

Oral disc · Tentacle · Mouth · Coelenteron (body cavity) · Pharynx · Corallites · Costae · Septa

...dodermis · Mesoglea · Ectodermis · Cilia · Cnidoblast (stinging cell) · Gonads · Mesenteries · Coenosteum · Wall · Columella · Paliform lobes

Coral anatomy.

Soft corals, such as this Sarcophyton, may grow to a considerable size.

Taxonomical Charts

The Phylum Cnidaria

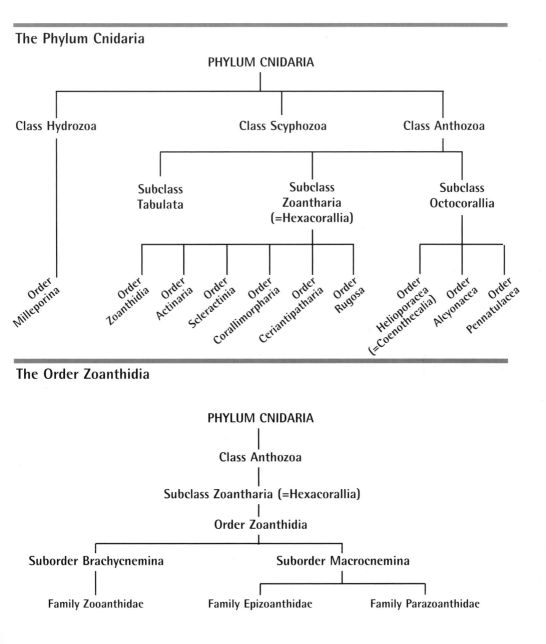

The Order Zoanthidia

The Order Scleractinia

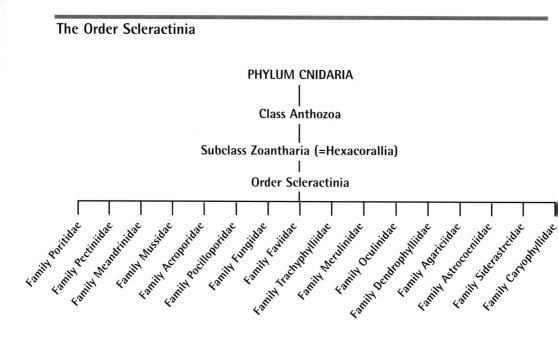

PHYLUM CNIDARIA
|
Class Anthozoa
|
Subclass Zoantharia (=Hexacorallia)
|
Order Scleractinia

Family Poritidae
Family Pectiniidae
Family Meandrinidae
Family Mussidae
Family Acroporidae
Family Pocilloporidae
Family Fungiidae
Family Faviidae
Family Trachyphylliidae
Family Merulinidae
Family Oculinidae
Family Dendrophylliidae
Family Agariciidae
Family Astrocoeniidae
Family Siderastreidae
Family Caryophylliidae

The Order Corallimorpharia

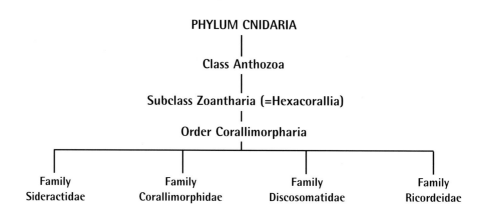

PHYLUM CNIDARIA
|
Class Anthozoa
|
Subclass Zoantharia (=Hexacorallia)
|
Order Corallimorpharia

Family
Sideractidae

Family
Corallimorphidae

Family
Discosomatidae

Family
Ricordeidae

The Order Helioporacea (=Coenothecalia)

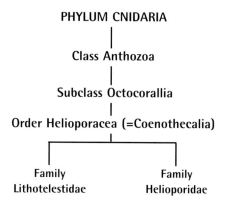

PHYLUM CNIDARIA

Class Anthozoa

Subclass Octocorallia

Order Helioporacea (=Coenothecalia)

Family Lithotelestidae   Family Helioporidae

The Order Alcyonacea

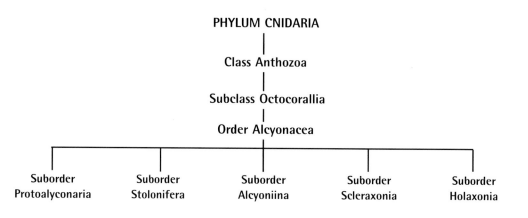

PHYLUM CNIDARIA

Class Anthozoa

Subclass Octocorallia

Order Alcyonacea

Suborder Protoalyconaria   Suborder Stolonifera   Suborder Alcyoniina   Suborder Scleraxonia   Suborder Holaxonia

Herpolitha *is known as "slipper coral."*

The Suborder Stolonifera

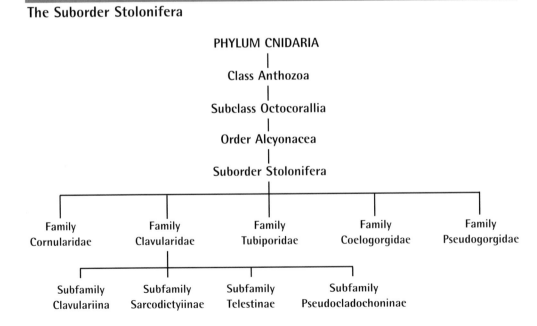

PHYLUM CNIDARIA
|
Class Anthozoa
|
Subclass Octocorallia
|
Order Alcyonacea
|
Suborder Stolonifera

| Family Cornularidae | Family Clavularidae | Family Tubiporidae | Family Coelogorgidae | Family Pseudogorgidae |

| Subfamily Clavulariina | Subfamily Sarcodictyiinae | Subfamily Telestinae | Subfamily Pseudocladochoninae |

Nemenzophyllia has been dubbed "fox coral" for no obvious reason.

The Suborder Alcyoniina

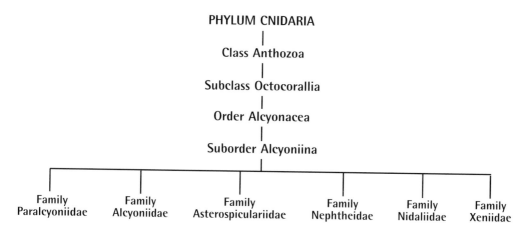

PHYLUM CNIDARIA

Class Anthozoa

Subclass Octocorallia

Order Alcyonacea

Suborder Alcyoniina

Family Paralcyoniidae   Family Alcyoniidae   Family Asterospiculariidae   Family Nephtheidae   Family Nidaliidae   Family Xeniidae

The Suborder Scleraxonia

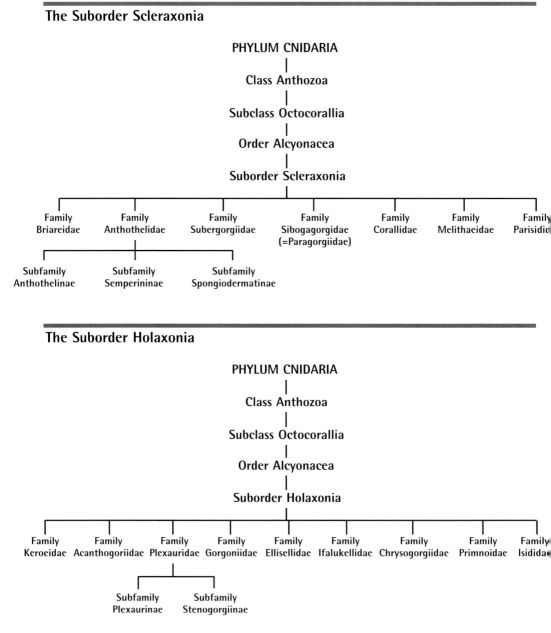

PHYLUM CNIDARIA

Class Anthozoa

Subclass Octocorallia

Order Alcyonacea

Suborder Scleraxonia

Family Briareidae

Family Anthothelidae

Family Subergorgiidae

Family Sibogagorgidae (=Paragorgiidae)

Family Corallidae

Family Melithaeidae

Family Parisidid

Subfamily Anthothelinae

Subfamily Semperininae

Subfamily Spongiodermatinae

The Suborder Holaxonia

PHYLUM CNIDARIA

Class Anthozoa

Subclass Octocorallia

Order Alcyonacea

Suborder Holaxonia

Family Keroeidae

Family Acanthogoriidae

Family Plexauridae

Family Gorgoniidae

Family Ellisellidae

Family Ifalukellidae

Family Chrysogorgiidae

Family Primnoidae

Family Isidida

Subfamily Plexaurinae

Subfamily Stenogorgiinae

INFORMATION

Information is the key to success with any marine aquarium, and is especially important for an aquarist with an interest in corals. The following resources should answer most questions and provide access to still more detailed information through links and bibliographic citations.

Internet Sites

For subscribers to America Online: Keyword AQUARIUM provides links to major public aquarium web sites.

Go to Keyword HOBBIES, then select "Aquarium Science" from the menu to access the aquarium hobby message board.

For subscribers to Compuserve Information Service: GO FISHNET accesses the huge forum for aquarists, both freshwater and marine, including a library of indispensable information on a host of topics.

Newsgroups

✔ *news.alt.aquaria*
✔ *news.rec.aquaria*
✔ *news.sci.aquaria*

Numerous list servers and on-line discussion groups for reef aquarists exist.

For example, sending e-mail to *majordomo@ iList.net* with the message "subscribe reef-l" will place you on this mailing list for reef aquarium hobbyists. Copies of e-mail sent to *reef-l@iList. net* are distributed to each subscriber on the list. Other lists work the same way.

Periodicals

Each of these periodicals contains articles relevant to the maintenance of corals in aquariums. Some are devoted solely to this subject.

SeaScope
Aquarium Systems, Inc.
8141 Tyler Boulevard
Mentor, OH 44060

Journal of Maquaculture
Breeder's Registry
P.O. Box 255373
Sacramento, CA 95865

Aquarium Fish Magazine
Fancy Publications
P.O. Box 6050
Mission Viejo, CA 92690

Coral Reef, Reef Encounter
International Society for Reef Studies
Dr. John Ogden
Florida Institute of Oceanography
830 First Street S
St. Petersburg, FL 33701

Ocean Realm
4067 Broadway
San Antonio, TX 78209

Freshwater and Marine Aquarium Magazine
RCM Publications
144 West Sierra Madre Boulevard
Sierra Madre, CA 91024

Tropical Fish Hobbyist
TFH Publications, Inc.
One TFH Plaza
Neptune, NJ 07753

Other Sites to Visit Using any Web Browser

Aquarium Frontiers Online
(An online magazine for freshwater
and marine aquarists, usually devoted
to advanced topics.)
http://www.aquariumfrontiers.com/default.asp

Breeder's Registry
(A web site for propagators of marine
fish and invertebrates.)
http://www.actwin.com/fish/br/index.html

Center for Marine Conservation *http://www.cmc-ocean.org*

Coral Reef Alliance *http://www.coral.org*

Coral Reef Task Force *http://coralreef.gov/trade.html*

Ecovitality *http://www.ecovitality.org*

Geothermal Aquaculture Research
Foundation
http://www.garf.org

Harbor Branch Oceanographic
Institute
http://www.hboi.org

Marine Aquarium Council *http://www.aquariumcouncil.org*

Online Reef Aquarist Society *http://www. panix.com/~cmo1/reef/*

Reeflink *http://www. reeflink.com*

Aquarists with an interest in taxonomy could hardly choose a better place to start than
the University of Arizona's "Tree of Life" web site: *http://ag.arizona.edu/tree/phylogeny.html*
This site also contains a links page: *http://ag.arizona.edu/tree/home.pages/links.html*
Aquarists can follow the links to ferret out additional sites devoted to a variety of specialized
taxonomic interests.

Books

The selections included here are the most recent and comprehensive works on corals in the aquarium, general information on minireef aquariums, and related topics. All feature bibliographic information that should provide even greater access to the vast literature on corals and their aquarium care.

Delbeek, J. C. and J. Sprung. *The Reef Aquarium, Volume One.* Coconut Grove, Florida: Ricordea Publishing, 1994.

Fossa, S. and A. J. Nielsen. *The Modern Coral Reef Aquarium, Vol. 1.* Bornheim, Germany: Birgitt Schmettkamp Verlag, 1996.

Green, Edmund and Frances Shirley. *The Global Trade in Coral. WCMC Biodiversity Series No. 9.* Cambridge, United Kingdom: WCMC-World Conservation Press, 1999.

Heslinga, G., T. C. Watson, and T. Isama. *Giant Clam Farming.* Honolulu: Pacific Fisheries Development Foundation (NMFS/NOAA), 1990.

Swiftia, a striking non-photosynthetic gorgonian from the Caribbean, must be fed daily.

Kaplan, E. H. *A Field Guide to Coral Reefs of the Caribbean and Florida*. Boston, Massachusetts: Houghton-Mifflin Company, 1982.

Myers, Robert F. *Micronesian Reef Fishes*. Guam: Coral Graphics, 1989.

Sprung, J. and Charles Delbeek. *The Reef Aquarium, Volume Two*. Coconut Grove, Florida: Ricordea Publishing, 1994.

Tullock, John. *Natural Reef Aquariums*, 2nd ed. Shelburne, Vermont: Microcosm, 1999.

_____. *Clownfishes and Sea Anemones*. Hauppauge, New York: Barron's Educational Series, Inc., 1998.

Veron, J.E.N. *Corals of Australia and the Indo-Pacific*. North Ryde, NSW, Australia: Angus and Robertson, 1986.

I N D E X

Photo Credits

Paul Humann: pages 2–3, 4, 8 top, 8 bottom, 12 top, 12 bottom, 13 bottom, 21, 24, 25, 28, 32, 33 top left, 33 top right, 36, 40, 41, 44 top, 45 bottom, 52 top left, 52 top right, 52 bottom left, 52 bottom right, 53 left, 53 right, 56 top, 56 bottom left, 57 bottom left, 60 top right, 60 bottom right, 61 bottom right, 64 top left, 64 top right, 64 bottom left, 64 bottom right, 65 top left, 65 top right, 65 bottom left, 65 bottom right, 68 bottom right, 69, 80, 84, 88, 93; Scott W. Michael: pages 9 top, 9 bottom, 13 top, 29, 33 bottom, 44 bottom left, 44 bottom right, 45 top, 48, 57 top left, 57 top right, 57 bottom right, 60 top left, 60 bottom left, 61 top left, 61 top right, 61 bottom left, 68 top left, 68 top right, 68 bottom left, 72, 76, 77 top, 77 bottom, 89; Aaron Norman: page 16.

Cover Photos

Aaron Norman.

Important Notes

Electrical equipment for aquarium care is described in this book. Please do not fail to read the note below, since otherwise serious accidents could occur.

Water damage from broken glass, overflowing, or tank leaks cannot always be avoided. Therefore you should not fail to take out insurance.

Please take special care that neither children nor adults ever eat any aquarium plants. It can cause substantial health injury. Fish medication should be kept away from children.

Safety Around the Aquarium

Water and electricity can lead to dangerous accidents. Therefore you should make absolutely sure when buying equipment that it is also really suitable for use in an aquarium.

✔ Every technical device must have the UL sticker on it. These letters give the assurance that the safety of the equipment has been carefully checked by experts and that "with ordinary use" (as the experts say) nothing dangerous can happen.

✔ Always unplug any electrical equipment before you do any cleaning around or in the aquarium.

✔ Never do your own repairs on the aquarium or the equipment if there is something wrong with it. As a matter of principle, all repairs should only be carried out by an expert.

About the Author

John H. Tullock is one of North America's leading proponents of environmentally sound aquarium keeping. A native of Tennessee, Tullock received a Master of Science degree in 1979. He is the founder of one of the country's largest mail order suppliers of live organisms for marine aquariums.

Now a full-time author and consultant, Tullock has written six previous books and numerous magazine articles. His work has appeared in *Aquarium Fish Magazine, Aquarium Frontiers Online, Freshwater and Marine Aquarium Magazine*, and other hobbyist and trade publications.

All inquiries should be addressed to:
Barron's Educational Series, Inc.
250 Wireless Boulevard
Hauppauge, NY 11788
http://www.barronseduc.com

International Standard Book No. 0-7641-1203-1

Library of Congress Catalog Card No. 99-59661

Library of Congress Cataloging-in-Publication Data
Tullock, John H., 1951–
     Corals: everything about purchase, care, nutrient requirements, and setting up a coral aquarium / John Tullock.
          p.   cm. – (A complete pet owner's manual)
     Includes bibliographical references.
     ISBN 0-7641-1203-1 (alk. paper)
     1. Corals. 2. Marine aquariums. I. Title. II. Series.
SF458.C64 T86   2000
639.34'2–dc21   99-59661
                                                                CIP

Printed in Hong Kong

9 8 7 6 5 4 3 2